Arms and the Woman:

The Shattered Glass Ceiling

Arms and the Woman:

The Shattered Glass Ceiling

Maj Gen VK Shrivastava, VSM (Retd)

Vij Books India Pvt Ltd
New Delhi (India)

Published by

Vij Books India Pvt Ltd
(Publishers, Distributors & Importers)
2/19, Ansari Road
Delhi – 110 002
Phones: 91-11-43596460, 91-11-47340674
M: 98110 94883
E-mail: contact@vijpublishing.com
Web : www.vijbooks.in

Copyright © 2022, *Author*

ISBN: 978-93-93499-33-2 (Paperback)

All rights reserved.

No part of this book may be reproduced, stored in a retrieval system, transmitted or utilized in any form or by any means, electronic, mechanical, photocopying, recording or otherwise, without the prior permission of the copyright owner. Application for such permission should be addressed to the publisher.

The views expressed in this book are of the author in his personal capacity.

Cover and concept by
Rohan Sharma, MA Graphic Design, UAL, @itskrukd

Dedicated to

All women

Who are changing the way the world perceives them

Contents

Preface		ix
List of Abbreviations		xi
Chapter - 1	"The Coming into Being of The Glass Ceiling": An Interpretive Commentary on The Evolution of The Gender Roles	1
Chapter - 2	"Those Who Defied The Glass Ceiling": Women Warriors of the Yore	12
Chapter - 3	"A Gentle Knock On The Glass Ceiling": Tiptoeing into the Field of Arms	21
Chapter - 4	"Cracking The Glass Ceiling": Women in Uniform in the Two World Wars	28
Chapter - 5	"The Cracked Glass Ceiling": About Women Bearing Arms Against the State	38
Chapter - 6	"The Crumbling Glass Ceiling": About Women Bearing Arms for the State	48
Chapter - 7	"The Broken Glass Ceiling": Women in The Armed Forces, The Global Scene	60
Chapter - 8	"The Shattered Glass Ceiling": Women in The Armed Forces, The Indian Scene	69
Chapter – 9	Women in Combat Role: A Holistic Résumé of Reservations and Concerns	76
Chapter – 10	The New Eve: An Afterword	86

Appendices

Appendix A	The Woman	97
Appendix B	Ballad in Praise of Private Clarke	99
Appendix C	A Brief Explanation of Some of the Terms of Low-Intensity Conflicts	100
Appendix D	Actual Strength of Women (All Ranks) in Various Units/Branches of Indian Civil Police (As on January 1, 2020)	103
Appendix E	Actual Strength of Women (All Ranks) in India's Central Armed Police Forces (As on January 1, 2020)	104
Appendix F	There are No Gender-Neutral Battlefields	105
Bibliography		107
Index		113

Preface

Gender roles signify social order – well-established norms and expectations from men and women based on their sex. Surprisingly, minor differences apart, all the cultures were discriminatory towards women on this count. Only some of those biased determinants were biological, while all others were imposed by men who dominated public life. At no stage, women were in a position to define their own roles. Though the subtle forms of inequality continue to exist, backed by the fast pace of globalization and the push of information technology, their position and status at home and in society are fast changing. Whereas the process of transformation has many facets, this book encapsulates gender roles and biases strictly in the context of women and the profession of arms.

The opening chapter leads a reader down some less travelled byways of history and presents the evolution of gender roles from ancient to the present times. In that, the bearing of arms and warfare had remained strictly a male preserve. And yet, there were women in every era – admittedly very few and far apart – who had defied the well-entrenched conventions of their times and had taken to arms. There have been instances of military transvestism too – women who had taken to the profession of arms disguised as men in pursuit of their own goals.

Subsequent chapters then sequentially trace women's march from their informal presence in the war zone as 'Camp Followers' to their formal entry as nurses, and from their large-scale presence and participation in the two world wars to the present, where they are leading combat units, commanding nuclear-powered aircraft carriers and are ruling the skies as fighter pilots.

Violent use of arms takes many forms spanning many fields. No wonder both the past and the present history are replete with instances where women have been part of the armed struggles against the state – hardcore members of the violent military groups as insurgents, terrorists, and suicide bombers. It is equally true that there is a very large number of women, other than those in the armed forces, who bear arms for the state – civil police, armed constabularies, and para-military forces – guarding borders and maintaining law and order.

One of the closing chapters analytically deals at length with the hotly debated topic of women in the combat role. The book closes with a summative commentary on the evolving status and role of women in society and aims to allow readers enough latitude to reflect on the issue with their own inquisitive minds.

I close with two points of clarification. First, for the most part, it is women scholars and activists who have researched and written on the subject of biased gender roles, inequality, women's empowerment, and the like. Without being a male feminist, I found this effort both revealing and satisfying. Second, while raising, presenting, or analyzing contentious issues, a conscious effort was made to ensure that my writings were not biased because of my background and experiences of close to four decades of all-male army days.

Lastly, I do hope that the readers will find the subject and its well-researched presentation interesting enough to remain engaged with the book and that, some of the facets reflected upon will find a permanent resting place in their migratory memory.

Noida

25 August 2022

V K Shrivastava

Major General (Retired)

List of Abbreviations

4GW	-	4th Generation Warfare.
AR	-	Assam Rifles.
ATS	-	Anti-Terrorism Squad.
ATS	-	Auxiliary Territorial Service.
BOP	-	Border Out Post.
BSF	-	Border Security Force.
CAPF	-	Central Armed Police Forces.
Capt	-	Captain.
CCP	-	Chinese Communist Party.
CEO	-	Chief Executive Officer.
CFA	-	Cease Fire Agreement.
CISF	-	Central Industrial Security Force.
CPI (M)	-	Communist Party of India (Maoist).
CRPF	-	Central Reserve Police Force.
EIC	-	East India Company.
FANY	-	First Aid Nursing Yeomanry.
Gen	-	General.
IDF	-	Israel Defense Forces.
INA	-	Indian National Army.
ITBP	-	Indo-Tibetan Border Force.

LoC	-	Line of Control.
LTTE	-	Liberation Tigers of Tamil Eelam.
NDA	-	National Defence Academy.
NGO	-	Non-Government Organization.
PAF	-	Pakistan Air Force.
PC	-	Permanent Commission.
PLA	-	People's Liberation Army.
P M	-	Prime Minister.
POW	-	Prisoner of War.
QAIMNS	-	Queen Alexandra's Imperial Military Nursing Service.
RIMC	-	Rashtriya Indian Military College.
RN	-	Royal Navy.
Rs	-	Rupees.
SC	-	Supreme Court.
SSC	-	Short Service Commission.
ULFA	-	United Liberation Front of Assam.
US	-	United States.
USA	-	United States of America.
WAAC	-	Women's Army Auxiliary Corps.
WAC	-	Women's Auxiliary Corps.
WRAF	-	Women's Royal Air Force.
WRNS	-	Women's Royal Navy Service.
WW-I	-	World War - I.
WW-II	-	World War - II.

CHAPTER - 1

"THE COMING INTO BEING OF THE GLASS CEILING": AN INTERPRETIVE COMMENTARY ON THE EVOLUTION OF THE GENDER ROLES

"For most of history, anonymous was a woman."

- Virginia Woolf - A modernist English writer

Setting the Stage

Genetic studies offer clear insight into sexual dimorphism – the reasons why males and females of the same species differ in so many ways. In some of the species, it is more pronounced than in others. Nature has it that it is invariably the males who indulge in courtship rituals while it is the females who choose the mating partners. Therefore, dimorphism, besides making males typically heavier and stronger in build, usually also endows them with some additional adornments – mane, antlers, plumages, *et al* – to help them attract females for mating. Notably, however, in no way do the males of the species – whether the solitary territorial males or the Alfa-males of the herds or the packs – inflict themselves on the females. In short, in the animal kingdom, there is gender equality in the manner of their existence.

Unlike the animal world, however, the evolution of human beings scripts a different story altogether. From prehistoric to modern times, the progression has remained heavily weighted against women, as the following narration would illustrate. By design, the text dwells at length on ancient times and old civilizations since those societies established the gender roles and set the tone for the growing discriminatory attitude and practices against women in due course. The text retains an Indo-centric focus.

A Global Survey of the Era Gone By

In the Paleolithic [1] period, early humans lived in caves, in small groups, and were hunters and gatherers. They used rather rough and ready stone tools for hunting and led a nomadic life in search of game and food. Archeological finds, and research works of paleontologists and anthropologists, have convincingly established that in the prehistoric stone age, despite their natural differences, men and women were by and large equals in the division of labour – that of hunting and gathering – quite contrary to the common belief that it was essentially the man who hunted. Excavations in South America's Andean heights of the mid-twentieth century reconfirmed that the women of the era were hunters too. [2] By interpolation, therefore, women were also fishing and trapping routinely alongside their male counterparts besides gathering of course. Indeed, tribal women, whether in the deep interiors of Amazon or of the *Jarawa* tribe of the Andaman Islands, are doing so even today.

Admittedly, hunting was harder and riskier than gathering, and the compulsions of childbearing and nursing must have restricted women's hunting forays. Men, therefore, must have hunted more often, though not exclusively. Even so, surprisingly, all the cave art of the era had traditionally depicted only scruffy burly men carrying a club, making tools, or hunting. Inadvertently, those imaginative renderings by the cave artists of the yore – males most likely – have left behind the earliest signs of the emerging gender roles.

The Neolithic era, or the New Stone Age, saw the beginning of agriculture and the domestication of plants and animals. The period also saw the dawn of pottery making and weaving. These changes led to an incredible transformation in the lifestyles of early humans. Enabled and provided by such means, they soon settled down in larger groups around fertile lands and perennial water sources. The greater permanency of the settlements also brought women's domestic skills to the fore. Their pre-and post-natal needs, and their child-rearing duties, influenced the gradual emergence of their role as homemakers and gatherers while men hunted – to a much lesser degree by then – tended fields and herded cattle to take on the role of providers. In due course, it also became necessary to protect the settlements – the land, home and hearth, womenfolk, and the livestock – from the foraging rival groups. That too became a man's job being hardier of the two sexes. The arrangement, resulting from men's natural advantages, marked the origin of their responsibility to bear arms. In the process, as protectors and providers, they took on a more dominating role.

With the advent of metallurgy, the Neolithic Age gave way to the Bronze Age and the stone tools and weapons made way for the more sophisticated metal ones. The transition also witnessed the revolutionary invention of the wheel. Interestingly, it was first used as a potter's wheel and not for any means of transportation. Admittedly ox-drawn carts were invented soon enough. Be that as it may, the cumulative effect resulted in large-scale urbanization and coming into being of Bronze Age cultures – organized communities living in city-states with their own set of religious beliefs, trade practices, and social order. In the context of this chapter, it is the last aspect of the 'social order' that needs to be explored in some detail to establish how these defined women's status and role in society. To that end, some of the ancient civilizations – Mesopotamian, Roman, Egyptian, and of course, the one in the Indus Valley – are being subjected to some scrutiny. Following narration would illustrate how each of these civilizations, despite their time and space separations, had systematically discriminated against women and distorted the aspect of gender equality forever.

Mesopotamian Civilization, arguably the earliest of them all, had evolved into a patriarchal system wherein women were respected and treated well. However, the education of a girl child was not encouraged, early arranged marriage was the norm for young women and, once married, they were generally expected to remain happily engaged as homemakers. Weaving was one of the few vocations they could pursue at home or outside. Their religious practices did allow women to become priestesses who in turn were expected to indulge in religious prostitution with the male priests, and so also others who may seek such favours, 'to spread divine fertility'. Whatever may have been the justifying logic behind this practice, it does signify women's sexual subjugation in a male-dominated society – under the garb of a religious ritual in the instant case.

In the Roman world too, women were disadvantaged on many counts. For example, though they were citizens of the state, they had no voting rights. Stretching the point further, they had no role to play in politics, had no say in public life, and were by and large confined to their homely duties. Admittedly, some of those from influential families did pull strings from the wings and wielded power. In general, however, only those from the lower classes worked outside their homes. There was also a dress code for women signifying the section of the society they belonged to – the privileged upper crust or the lower strata. In legal terms too, Roman women were less equal to men. For, though both the sons and the daughters had equal rights to inherit property, women had to nominate a male member to act on their behalf because of their assumed *infermitas consilii* – infirmity in judgment. Roman attitude towards women was best described by Emperor Augustus when he said, "Nature has made it so that we cannot live with them particularly comfortably, but we can't live without them at all." [3]

Like the Romans, Greek women had no voting rights either. Similarly, like their Roman counterparts, they too could not administer their own property without the oversight of a male family member. Even Aristotle, the learned Greek philosopher whose thoughts on matters of social justice were way ahead of his times, is said to have had doubts about women's worldly wisdom. In his well-known work, *Politics,* he states "The relation of male to female is by nature a relation of superior to inferior and ruler to ruled." In any case, centuries before Aristotle, the Greek epic Iliad gave an indication of the gender roles when Homer proclaimed, 'War will be men's business.'

In comparison, women in the Egyptian Civilization were far less discriminated against. They were treated as equal to men on all counts except in the domain of occupation – it was men who ruled, held positions of authority in public life, and formed the soldiery. Those restrictions apart, women enjoyed much independence and other privileges – they could marry by choice, initiate their own divorce proceedings, hold and administer their property independently, do business, enter into agreements, depose in the courts of law, and could also become respected priestesses. Not surprisingly, therefore, when the situation so demanded, quite a few of the Egyptian queen-mothers and queens rose to be pharaohs and ruled for long before handing over the reins to the next legal male successor.

The fact that all the aforesaid civilizations adored women is apparent from the fact that they all had female goddesses. Ishtar, the goddess of love and sexuality, was one of the most important ones for the Mesopotamians. Isis, one of the many Egyptian goddesses, symbolized fertility and motherhood. Romans also worshipped many goddesses. Minerva, the goddess of wisdom, and Venus, the goddess of love were some of them. Greeks, too, had quite a few of them – Artemis, the goddess of the hunt, and Nike, the goddess of victory, to name a few. It is important to note that while most of them were worshipped, some were also derided for all the ills of the world. For example, Greek mythology depicts Pandora as the harbinger of all the ills and snake-haired Medusa as a winged female monster.

As a digression, it may be of interest to know that the rounded-off tick mark-like logo of the well-known shoe brand Nike is the exact replica of the design emblazoned on the waistband buckle of the goddess Nike.

The Indian Scene

Returning to the point of digression, it is time to take a deeper look at the scene in ancient India where three continuous yet distinct periods, stretching from around 3000 BCE to 500 CE, emphatically defined the role and the status of women in India. It is being dealt with at some length since Indians proudly relate to the inheritances of their continuing civilization and those deep-seated impulses of the yore have continued to influence their ideas of gender roles ever since.

First, the Indus Valley Civilization (3000 BCE - 1500 BCE) that had flourished on the banks of the Indus River. Whereas literary evidence of the period is difficult to come by, the excavated remains point to a prosperous and well-organized society. Therein, in a largely egalitarian arrangement, women were essentially confined to the role of homemakers and caregivers. Hairstyles and the ornaments noticed on the terracotta figurines indicate that women were both admired and indulged. Some of the female bronze statuettes also point to women's engagement in such performing arts as dancing and music. The civilization is not known to have been engaged in any soldierly pursuits, or in any internal or external conflict, and gradually succumbed to a spate of natural disasters.

Second, the Vedic period that followed (1500 BCE - 500 BCE) can be said to have laid the foundation of the Indian civilization on many counts – it saw the emergence of Hinduism as a religion and the caste system for example. *Vedas* and the *Upanishads* also find their origin in this period. More importantly, the era had held the most prescriptive sway on all aspects of women's social standing. It had aggrandized and curtailed their status in equal measure if not more of the latter. The following text dilates the point.

In the Vedic time, women had considerable equality and freedom in society. "Historical studies and the scriptures indicate that Indian women enjoyed a comparatively high status during the early Vedic period, surpassing contemporary civilizations in ancient Greece and Rome." [4] There was no restriction on their academic pursuits. Not surprisingly, many parts and hymns of Rig-Veda, the oldest scripture that humanity possesses, are attributed to women writers - Maitreyi and Gargi to name a few. Indeed, during the Vedic time, domestic life was in no way inconsistent with spiritual life. [5]

The custom of *Swayamwara* allowed women to choose their husbands from amongst the competing suitors. The custom of *Gandharva Vivah* allowed even live-in relationships – something that even the present-day society is trying to get accustomed to. Widows could re-marry too. A wife had an authoritative say in family matters and played a prominent role in all religious functions. Hindu mythology had also placed women on a high pedestal and had vested goddesses with quite a few divine powers – Laxmi was the goddess of wealth, Durga that of *Shakti* (power), and Saraswati the goddess of learning and knowledge. Even as the consorts of the male gods they were depicted as influencers cum conscious keepers and therefore equally important. For example, while performing *Homa* or *Havan* (a ritual of making offerings into a consecrated fire), each offering ends with '*Swaha*' – the name of *Agni*'s wife, the God of Fire.

But for all that, the Hindu scriptures of that period had laid down in great detail the "Four ends of a man", specifying a man's obligations for his final emancipation, but were absolutely silent on a woman's journey through her life for similar attainment. *Manusmrity*,[6] meaning 'Manu's Musings' or 'Manu's Code', reflects the Vedic view of the society and lays down the rights, duties, laws *et al* governing the Hindu way of life. Therein, with regard to the women "On one hand, it is enjoined that she should be shown utmost respect, on the other hand, she is said to deserve no freedom."[7] As per the established social norms, a girl child was to be brought up by her father, protected and provided for by her husband upon being married and was to be looked after by the son(s) in the event of her husband's death. While the arrangement must be lauded for ensuring women's wellbeing, it must also be faulted for making them male-dependent – de facto curtailing their independence.

Manusmrity had ordained that, with marriage, a woman was to obediently submit to her husband in totality. A young bride was advised never to annoy her husband. As a wife, she became an *Ardhangini* – husband's complimenting half – and was thus expected to willingly give up her own individuality and identity. She was not supposed to be in the forefront or to excel but was expected to remain in the background and devote her time and talent to her husband's cause. Epic *Ramayana* projects Sita as an ideal woman who remains dutifully devoted to her husband, Rama, even after she was subjected to *Agni Pariksha* – trial by fire – and banishment to the forest. Worse still, *Mahabharat* glorifies Draupadi for submissively facing the ignominy of polyandry for no fault of hers. Note the lack of women's voices in both these epics. Such portrayals only advanced the flawed notion that a wife must suffer and sacrifice more for the good of the family. With the passage of time, the idea got deeply ingrained.

The third and the last of the three periods under review relates to the waning of the Vedic times coinciding with the waxing of the civilization in the Gangetic Plains (500 BCE - 500 CE). If the Vedic way of life was prescriptive on women and their role, what followed turned out to be even more restrictive for them. The period was deeply influenced by Kautilya's writings and "*Arthashastra* imposed more stigmas on women as Kautilya dismissed women's liberation and they were not free even to go elsewhere without husband's permission." [8]

In the contextual framework of this narration tracing the evolution of gender roles, an important and continuing strain of ancient India must be taken note of. That being, both *Ramayana* and *Mahabharat* provide the earliest references to warfare and in both of them, only men were engaged in the trials of combat. Similarly, the *Varna* system – the social order of the Vedic times – had designated *Kshatriyas* as the warrior class and only men folk were supposed to bear arms to protect the society. It may be recalled that before the commencement of fighting in *Mahabharat*, Lord Krishna had to remind Arjun of his manly duty to wage a righteous war as a *Kshatriya* warrior prince. Lastly, the civilization in the Gangetic Plains had flourished under the empire builders where only men formed the soldiery. In short, in India, the profession of arms had remained strictly a male prerogative.

Lest it is lost sight of it must be mentioned that both the Romans and the Greeks were also empire builders and had maintained large standing armies. However, just like in ancient India, it was only men who made up the Roman legions or the Greek phalanx. In China too, the body of troops had only men.

A Brief on Medieval to the Present Times

In the thousand years of medieval times, that is, from the 6th to the 16th century, India experienced numerous incursions from the Arabs, Turks, Afghans, and eventually, the Mughals who went on to establish their dynastic rule. It was a period of great cultural interaction. Regrettably, the era must be recorded as a 'Dark Age' when juxtaposed with women's rights and their role in society.

In the wake of the raiders and the invaders came their customs and tradition. Strict Islamic laws on veiling led to the *Purdah* system restricting women's social movement. Similar influences also prompted polygamy among the upper-class Hindus. It became common for the rulers and the nobles to have many wives, concubines, and slave girls in their *Harem* – exclusive quarters for women. Women came to be regarded as men's property. While men's privileges remained unfettered, those of the women were severely restrained. Re-marriage of widows was discouraged. A widow, considered inauspicious and shunned by society, was consigned to lead a lonely life of penance or was even expected to die on her husband's funeral pyre – the regressive yet aggrandized practice of *Sati*. Amongst the Rajputs, there was also the custom of *Jauhar* – en mass self-immolation. In the early fourteenth century, Padmini, the queen of Mewar, and many other women committed *Jauhar* to protect their honour when their husbands fought to the death in the battle they lost.

Admittedly, women were allowed fair liberty when it came to the luxury of personal grooming, cosmetics, perfumes, fine dressing, adornments *et al,* just as they were encouraged to pursue such art forms as singing and dancing – understandably so since it all pleased and entertained men. But they had no say or role outside the affairs of their households. Women from both the Hindu and the Muslim communities had been caged in a golden cage and their social status had sunk low. Indeed, a 16th-century couplet by renowned poet Tulsidas conveys society's strong undercurrents of a woman's place when he wrote *"Dhol, ganwar, shudra, pashu, nari, yeh sab tadan ke adhikari"* meaning 'a drum, an illiterate, one from the lower class, an animal and a woman are all entitled to beating'.

Cut to the more modern times and one finds that as recently as in the nineteenth century the so-called 'moderates' of gender equality were anything but that. "Always wary of the extremes, they reinforced the notion that women's role, position, status, and the identity revolved around the family and any reform that undermines that institution was an invitation to disaster." [9] Indeed, under one pretext or the other, women were even deprived of their voting rights.

Apparently, at no stage, a woman's true worth was ever understood, explored, or appreciated. See Appendix A for an ode that best describes her near-perfect persona.

Conclusion

The foregoing sweep of narration covering more than five millennia has presented how women's role and their social standing changed as the societies evolved – the onset of gendering so to say. Surprisingly, minor differences apart, all the cultures were discriminatory towards women. Only some of those biased determinants were biological while all others were imposed by men who dominated public life. Therefore, women were never in a position to define their own roles. In the process, most of the men's privileged superiority had come at the expense of women's unfair detriments. Thus, with the passage of time, social norms firmly confined women to household chores and restrained them in a variety of ways denying them opportunities to excel in other fields – the profession of arms being one of them. Soldiering had remained a man's calling. The glass ceiling was in place.

And yet, there were women in every era who had dared to break that glass ceiling. The next chapter traces the exploits of some of them.

Endnotes

1. The word, also spelt as Palaeolithic, literally means Old Stone (Age).

2. https://theprint.in/science/yes-she-did-new-findings-show-prehistoric-women-hunted-too/539043/ (Accessed on March 16, 2021.)

3. https://www.ancient.eu/article/659/the-role-of-women-in-the-roman-world/ (Accessed on April 1, 2021.)

4. Atasi Mahapatra, *Gender equality and ancient Indian culture: A study*, International Journal of Humanities and Social Science Invention (IJHSSI), Volume 7 Issue 08 Ver. III, |August 2018, PP 22.

5. S K Pandit, *Women in Society*, Rajat Publications, New Delhi, 1998, pp 3.

6. It was translated by the British philologist Sir William Jones in 1776 and was later used by the British to frame the Hindu Law in India

7. Ainslie T Embree (Ed), *Sources of Indian Tradition*, second edition, Penguin Books India (P) Ltd, 1991, pp 228.

8. Naresh Rout, *Role of Women in Ancient India*, Odisha Review, Jan 2016, pp 42.

9. Helena Rosenblatt, *The Lost History of Liberalism : From Ancient Rome to the Twenty-First Century*, Princeton University Press, 2018, pp 239.

CHAPTER - 2

"THOSE WHO DEFIED THE GLASS CEILING": WOMEN WARRIORS OF THE YORE

Defined by no man, you are your own story,
Blazing through the world, turning history into her story.

- Nikita Gill - Indian poet and writer
(From "An Ode to Fearless Women")

The Backdrop

The previous chapter has highlighted that in all the ancient cultures, women had no role to play when it came to skill at arms or warfare. It was a male preserve and therefore, history too tends to be men oriented. Even so, mythology, folklore, and fairy tales are full of fascinating and romantic stories of women warriors. Lost in the pages of history are also daring exploits of women who had defied the well-entrenched conventions of their times and had taken to arms – either forced by circumstances or inspired by their righteous convictions. Though few and far apart, they were all spirited women whose deeds on the battlefields had made them heroines nonpareil. While some of them belonged to the ruling elite, many others were from more humble backgrounds. Interestingly, some of them, for personal reasons, had even masqueraded as men to enlist and had successfully pursued their soldierly careers for long years in all-male units. In all cases, besides being a good daughter, a devoted wife, or a doting mother, they all had risen to the occasion and had also proved their mettle as warriors.

The following passages briefly recount heroic deeds of only some of them from the ancient and medieval times – from different cultures and from far-off places. The remarkable determination of those who had impersonated men in pursuit of their personal goals makes fascinating reading. By design, the Indian women warriors being presented have been picked from the more recent past, and their actions have been presented in greater detail.

For Whom the Bell Tolls

The first one from the distant past is Queen Fu Hao. She was a high priestess and one of the many wives of Emperor Wu Ding, who ruled China around 1200 BCE. She broke all existing traditions to take on the role of a military commander with as many as 13,000 troops under command. Though not many details of her ventures have survived, she is known to have fought many battles and was considered one of the most powerful military leaders of her time. She also had her own fiefdom adjoining the empire. Her tomb was discovered only in 1975 and the presence of many weapons and other artifacts buried alongside indicated both her royal and military status.

Greek Queen Artemisia – named after the Greek goddess of 'Hunt', Artemis – provides arguably the earliest recorded example of a woman warrior. She is also perhaps the only one who had made her mark on the high seas.

Consequent to her husband's death Artemisia ascended the throne as the queen of the small city-state called Halicarnassus – present-day Bodrum in Turkey. As an astute ruler, she allied with Xerxes, the King of Persia, and fought against some smaller island city-states of the Greeks. In the battle of Artemisium, she was in personal command of her fleet of five warships. A little later, in 480 BCE, she excelled in the naval battle of Salamis to snatch victory from the jaws of defeat. Factual accounts of her battles, and of her personal dare-devilry were recorded by Herodotus [1] in his book *Histories*.

Zenobia was the queen of the Palmyrene kingdom – an eastern province of the Roman Empire, generally in the region close to present-day Syria. Consequent to her husband's assassination, she declared herself the regent of her minor son. She was a warrior queen who led from the front and readily roughed it out with her soldiers on the battlefield. She extended her kingdom and, as an able administrator, held sway over the entire territory. Around 270 CE she invaded Egypt, suppressed an uprising there, and then seceded from Rome to declare herself the Empress of Palmyrene Empire. Angered by her audacity, the Roman Emperor marched against her. She was defeated, captured, and paraded through the streets of Rome in chains made of gold. Details about her final years have remained hazy but she is known to have died in 274 CE, aged 34. [2]

Suffice it to say that, other than those mentioned above, there were many others in the ancient world who had earned a name for themselves for their military leadership and for bravery on the battlefield. Be that as it may, this narrative of the distant past is being closed with an anecdote in a lighter vein. Plutarch, the famous Greek historian has recorded that King Pyrrhus, a fêted warlord of his time and a strong opponent of the Romans, was killed in a street battle when a woman bystander threw a roof tile that hit and stunned the King for a few moments giving enough opportunity to his opponents to kill him. She must go down as 'The woman soldier who never was'.

Coming to medieval times, there can be no better example than that of the famous French female warrior of the early 15th century, Joan of Arc. She was still in her teens when she played a key role in France's 'Hundred Year War' against the English. Her uncanny military ideas and moves greatly influenced the strategies of the French army. She was particularly instrumental in the French victory at Orléans and was nicknamed "The Maid of Orléans". Unfortunately, she was betrayed by some French nobles who were allied with the English and was captured. Tried for heresy by the English, she was declared guilty and burnt at stake in May 1430. She was only nineteen then. At the behest of the then Pope, her trial was re-examined in 1456 and she was found innocent. Later, in 1909, she was beatified and was canonized as a 'Saint' in 1920.

Though warfare has been mainly men's affair, there have been instances of military transvestism – women who had taken to the profession of arms disguised as men. One of the earliest recorded instances is that of Private Clarke, who fought alongside her husband for nine long years in the English Civil War of the 1640s. Her true gender was discovered only when she bore him a son while still in service. See Appendix B for the ballad written in 1655 that lauds her. There were many others like her and the following passages narrate the exploits of just two of them.

Christian Cavanagh was born in 1667 in Dublin, Ireland. She was a tomboy girl and excelled in riding. In due course, she got married to Richard Welsh,[3] who, in 1692, was forcibly enlisted in the army when in a drunken stupor. A year later she cut off her hair, got into her husband's baggy clothes, bought a sword for her, and joined the army as a dragoon – a mounted soldier – as Kit Welsh, to find her husband. Soon enough she was in action in Belgium, where she got injured and was captured. She was fortunate to be back in the regiment after the exchange of prisoners. However, she was discharged when she called out another soldier and killed him in a duel. Undaunted, she enrolled yet again in a different unit and continued her soldierly exploits. She was wounded once again. Nevertheless, it was in 1704 that she finally met her husband and the two decided to keep the secret and carry on with their soldiering. The twist in the tale came when Kit got severely wounded for the third time and the dressings of her multiple wounds led to her unmasking. She was discharged but was allowed to be with the unit either as an officer's cook or as a sutler – the versions differ. Her husband was killed in action in 1709. In due course, she married twice again to be widowed both times. In 1712, when she got wounded for the fourth time because of her uncalled-for meddling on the front line, she finally returned to England to live peacefully on her pension.

Kit Welsh was known in the unit as "The Pretty Dragoon" while her commanding officer called her "The Best Man I Had." She was buried with full military honours when she died in 1739. Her story which appeared a little later was authored by none other than Daniel Defoe of the *Robinson Crusoe* fame.

Exploits of Loreta Janeta Velázquez, a beautiful she-soldier, are also equally remarkable. She was an aggressively enterprising person and, quite unlike all the women warriors mentioned above, she not only fought as a combatant but also spun a web of her womanly charms as a spy. Born in Havana, Cuba, in 1842, she grew up in New Orleans, United States of America (USA). When the American Civil War broke out in 1861, she cross-dressed as a man – sporting mustaches and a beard for effect – and fought on in the Confederate Army as an 'independent soldier'. However, lusting for excitement and fame she surreptitiously crossed over into the Union Territory and then, dressed as a woman, travelled all the way to Washington. There she attended social functions, parties and struck conversations with the Union officers to gather intelligence. Having sneaked back to her own side, and having shared the enemy information, she was back into action. Despite her injuries in one of the clashes, her disguise held. To recover fully from her injuries, she went back to New Orleans where she lived as the woman that she actually was. Ironically, she was arrested there by her own side on charges of spying for the Union Army disguised as a woman. She was obliged to blow her cover and explain. Instead of the kudos that she expected she was given minor punishment for impersonation.

Undeterred, she enlisted once again and was wounded for the second time in action. When the required medical attention gave away her gender, she decided to hang her boots. However, bored by inactivity, she offered her services as a spy. After the Civil War was over, she wrote a book titled "*The Woman in Battle: A Narrative of the Exploits, Adventures, and Travels of Madame Loreta Janeta Velázquez; Otherwise Known as Lieutenant Harry T. Buford, Confederate States Army*". The book was dedicated to her Confederate comrades and has remained controversial ever since. Equally controversial are the details about her death – 1897 or 1923. [4]

With that, it is time to take a look at the Indian scene. Ancient Indian history cites many instances of queens who had ruled but none who may have also fought battles. However, there were many gallant warrior queens in medieval times. For example: -

- ➢ Rani Durgavati, the ruler of Gondwana (Present-day Nagpur-Vidarbha region), died on the battlefield repelling the Mughals.
- ➢ Tara Bai, the queen of the Maratha Empire in the early 18th century, is known to have led her forces, riding her white charger, to prevent Mughal incursions. [5]
- ➢ In the late 18th century Rani Velu Nachiyar of Sivaganga estate in southern India had challenged the 'sword in the arms trading' of the East India Company (EIC) and was surely the first one to have used a human bomb.
- ➢ Ahilya Bai Holkar, the Maratha ruler of Malwa region (West-Central India plateau) in the late 18th century, had successfully fought off the Mughals leading her army riding her war elephant.

While the Indians do admire the above-mentioned women warriors, it is the Rani Lakshmi Bai of Jhansi – the icon of India's First War of Independence, 1857 – whose patriotic zeal, steely resolve, and bravery they hold in the highest regard.

She was born in 1828 and excelled in riding and sword fighting in her childhood. She became queen of Jhansi when married to the king of that princely state. At the time of her husband's death in 1853, they had an adopted son. The British, in their bid to annex Jhansi, applied the 'Doctrine of Lapse,' [6] fixed a pension of Rupees (Rs) 60,000/- for Lakshmi Bai, and asked her to vacate Jhansi Fort which she did not. Smarting under the ignominy she started assembling her army.

When the rebellion started in May 1857, Jhansi had generally remained peaceful to start with. However, all hell broke loose when, in the first week of June, all the officers, ladies, and children of the Jhansi garrison were mercilessly killed by the rebellious sepoys. The British, who were already at loggerheads with the Rani, now marked her out for her suspected involvement in the massacre – tacit if not direct. Therefore, having suppressed the uprising and stabilized the situation, Company's forces under General (Gen) Rose marched on to Jhansi and, towards the end of March 1858, laid siege to the Jhansi Fort. When the Fort was stormed on April 3, 1858, Lakshmi Bai and her forces, though outnumbered and out-gunned, offered stiff resistance. Just before the Fort capitulated, Rani made good her escape – jumping off the high fort wall riding her horse as the folklore would have us believe – with a small force of her personal guards and joined the rebel forces at Kalpi, some 50 miles away. After a while, Gen Rose's forces advanced to Kalpi and captured it after a fierce battle that ensued towards the end of May 1858. Lakshmi Bai managed to slip away yet again and headed towards Gwalior to make it her new base for resistance. Hot on her heels Gen Rose caught up with Rani on the outskirts of Gwalior on June 17, 1858. Fighting British to the last, "Laksmi Bai, Rani of Jhansi – almost uniquely amongst the rebel leaders in the war – died in the saddle, sword in hand, commanding her troops." [7] In her admiration, Gen Rose is known to have said, "The Indian Mutiny had produced but one man, and that man was a woman." For the Indians, she remains an immortal brave heart.

Much later, Subhadra Kumari Chauhan, a well-known Indian poet, captured the moving account of Rani Lakshmi Bai's courageous fight, which became the rallying point during India's freedom struggle. Each stanza of the poem ends with the couplet *"Bundele harbloke muhn hamne suni Kahani thi, Khoob ladi mardani woh to Jhansi wali Rani thi."* Loosely translated it means "We heard the story from the mouths of Bundel bards, The one who fought on like men was the Queen of Jhansi." [8]

The saga of the Rani of Jhansi would be incomplete without a mention of valiant Jhalkari Bai who had joined the all-women unit of Lakshmi Bai's army and had risen to be her confidante. When the Jhansi Fort was stormed on April 3, 1858, she confused the British at the critical juncture of the battle by fighting on the ramparts of the Fort dressed as the Rani and thus facilitated the escape of Lakshmi Bai. Jhalkari Bai continued to rally her forces and died fighting the next day.

This inspiring account of Indian sheroes – she heroes – is being closed with the courageous efforts of another Lakshmi. Born in Madras (now Chennai) in 1914, Lakshmi Swaminathan grew up to be a doctor (Dr). In 1942 she moved to Singapore where she came in contact with Netaji Subhas Chandra Bose. Fired by her nationalistic fervor she readily agreed to Netaji's proposal to raise an all-women's regiment for the Indian National Army (INA). It was to be called 'Rani of Jhansi Regiment'. With that Dr Lakshmi became Captain (Capt) Lakshmi; a rank that stuck to her name all through though she rose to be a Colonel. [9]. Fighting alongside the Japanese forces, her regiment was in action near Imphal where she stood out both as a leader and a doctor. She was captured by the British in May 1945 but was released a year or so later. After independence, she remained active as a social worker and a doctor till her death in 2012.

As an aside, it is mentioned that INA had also recruited and trained 200 women to form its Chand Bibi Nursing Corps.

Conclusion

Imaginative folklores of women warriors tend to create the image of an all-conquering superwoman in our minds. True stories of gallant she soldiers further shore up our *idée fixe*. Be that as it may, the fact remains that in the recorded history of warfare spanning thousands of years, there have been many brave and ambitious women who had taken to arms against all the established norms of a patriarchal society. Motivated by their noble beliefs they all had defied the glass ceiling not as their first option, but as their last resort. They had realized that they had to and so they did. They never gave up easily. Even death had to fight them hard. Indeed, with their daring deeds, they all had shown their true colours even to the colour blinds.

Surprisingly, however, it was not the women's hard-fought battles that led to any shift in the long-established ideas about their role. It was their soft power that set the process in motion. Next chapter dwells on how it all started.

Endnotes

1. A Greek writer and a noted historian of that period. He too belonged to Halicarnassus. .

2. For more details of the foregoing female warriors visit https://www.thecollector.com/women-warriors-ancient-world. (Accessed on May 6, 2020).

3. Many accounts have also spelt the name as 'Walsh'.

4. For some more well researched details about she-soldiers see Jonathan Bastable, Antony Mason, Tony Allen (Ed), *Reader's Digest : Great Secrets of History*, Therefore Publishing House, Brighton, U K, 2014, pp 128-133.

5. For more details see Eaton, Richard M, *A Social History of the Deccan, 1300–1761: Eight Indian Lives*, Volume 1, Cambridge University Press, 2005, pp. 177–203.

6. Under the provisions of the 'Doctrine of Lapse', promulgated in 1847, East India Company could annex a princely state if the ruler had produced no heir.

7. Julian Spilsbury, *The Indian Mutiny*, Weidenfeld & Nicolson, London, 2007, pp 341.

8. Bundel refers to the central Indian region where she had fought the British.

9. Sehgal got added to her name consequent to her marriage to Col Prem Kumar Sehgal, a fellow officer in INA, in March 1947.

CHAPTER - 3

"A GENTLE KNOCK ON THE GLASS CEILING": TIPTOEING INTO THE FIELD OF ARMS

"In a gentle way, you can shake the world"

- Mahatma Gandhi.

Off the Record Presence of Women in the War Zones

In the past, warrior queens and she-soldiers apart, there have been women in the war zones who have played their part in sustaining war efforts – albeit informally and indirectly. The following passages briefly recount a few details about their role and their contributions.

All armies the world over have had 'Camp Followers', including the families of the officers and the men accompanying their husbands. However, in military parlance, the term generally refers to the civilians who do not officially belong to the organization but support it by providing such goods and services that the army does not in its bases and camps. Since these civilian service providers followed the army wherever it went, they came to be known as the camp followers. Amongst them were sutlers – civilian merchants – who traded in goods usually required by men besides also selling liquor. Occasionally they even advanced petty cash to the needy ones – admittedly for a consideration. Anyway, quite a few of them used to develop a marked degree of attachment and permanency with the units they roughed out with and catered to. [1]

Just for records, in the French Army, only soldiers' wives were formally allowed to be *cantinières* in the units to sell goods, eatables, and liquor to the troops.

Sutlers and *cantinières* apart, there were others who attended to such domestic chores of the officers and the men as cooking, washing, sewing, mending, and the likes for a fee. It was this second set of services that brought the women to the war zone. Quite often, few of them were wives of the serving soldiers who earned a little extra for the family while also remaining close to their husbands. At times some of those displaced in the war-torn countryside also sought to take refuge as camp followers but were not readily accepted to prevent enterprising spies from infiltrating. That apart, invariably there were prostitutes amongst the camp followers for good measure. Since all the camp followers, whatever their trade, had to be catered for and protected, armies did try to restrict their numbers. Even so, at times their numbers equaled or exceeded the size of the force itself. Mughals were perhaps the worst offenders on that count. "A Mughal army on the march resembled a mobile metropolis, with hundreds of tents and portable buildings divided into districts for the various line units - - - -." [2] It once also happened to the British when, after their disastrous campaign in Afghanistan, they decided to pull out from Kabul in 1842. "On Thursday, January 6th the march from Kabul began; there were about 4,500 fighting men and 12,000 followers." [3]

As can be well appreciated, the presence of this motley crowd of female followers always made the army's baggage train look a bit disorderly and tended to slow down the marches – they all were expected to march but quite a few often skirted the order (pun not intended) by riding the carts and the wagons on the sly. Occasionally they also created some disciplinary problems. Even so, force commanders had to take these aberrations in their stride since they were indispensable for the difference they made. Sadly, however, war records have rarely, if at all, made any references to these adventurous women or to their helping hand. It surely is a sad commentary on their contribution to the force.

Women camp followers got a semblance of formal recognition of their role during the American Revolutionary War (1775-1783) when the Continental Army under Gen George Washington started temporary enrolment of women not for their usual house-keeping tasks but for such duties as attending to the war-wounded or fetching water at the gun pits to cool the guns while firing. Therefore, unlike the other camp followers who were left behind in the rear areas, these 'Regimental Women' or 'Women of the Army', worked closer to the front alongside men. However, "It is important to observe here that women served *with*, not *in*, the armed forces during this time. That is, even though they may have been paid (or not paid) for the duties they performed, they did not hold military rank and were thus *attached to*, not a *part of*, the armed forces." [4] Exploits of one such brave woman merit a mention. Mary was the wife of cannoneer William Hays of the Continental Army. During the battle of Monmouth in June 1778 she saw her injured husband buckling down next to the canon he was loading. After quickly ascertaining that his injury was not serious, she, took up his place to load the canon and kept it in action throughout the battle. Her bravery and selfless action did not go unnoticed and was immediately granted field commission in the rank of sergeant. After the war, she was also entitled to the pension which she drew till her death in 1832.

The Small Beginnings

Women's informal role as above continued till the 1850s when the nursing services led to their formal entry into the profession of arms. Admittedly, even before that, there had been instances when female nurses had worked in army hospitals. For example, as early as 1664, a batch of nurses from St Thomas Hospital London had arrived in India and had served in the newly established hospital for the soldiers in Fort St George, Madras (now Chennai). However, these nurses had been 'loaned' and were neither a part of the army – whether in England or in India – nor were they deployed in the field. That happened only during the Crimean War (1853-1856) fought between the British and its allies against Russia. First-hand reporting from the war front by the British journalist William Howard Russell [5] about the harsh conditions and the lack of medical facilities led to public outcry and a demand for better professional care for the sick and the wounded.

In response, a group of nurses, including a few Catholic nuns under Florence Nightingale, were sent to help the overworked medical attendants and relieve the sufferings of the wounded in the hospitals. They arrived at Selimiye Barracks in Scutari (part of modern-day Istanbul) in November 1854. Florence Nightingale's selfless dedication to duty vastly improved the standards of patient care in the hospital. Often, when all others had retired for the night, she could be seen going around the wards. Not surprisingly, she soon earned the *sobriquet* 'Lady with the Lamp'. Her pioneering efforts and setting up of a school to train the nurses – Nightingale School for Nurses was the first-ever of its kind – attracted worldwide attention and admiration. She must be remembered as a legend in the profession of nursing and the leading lady who reformed military nursing and triggered the entry of women nurses into the armed forces.

Despite the impetus she provided, it was not until 1881 that the Army Nursing Service was established in England. It was named after Queen Victoria's daughter as Princess Christian's Army Nursing Service Reserve. "In 1884 a code of regulations for the 'Female Nursing Service' was drawn up. 1884 therefore marks the beginning of the overseas work of the sisters in military hospitals in peacetime." [6] In 1887 nurses accompanied the British forces to Egypt and to Sudan for better soldier care. Incidentally, nurses serving abroad were entitled to extra allowances and also to 'home leave' once during their tenure of duty.

It is noteworthy that the Russian nursing efforts during the Crimean War were also equally commendable. At the behest of the Russian Grand Duchess, a batch of 28 Russian 'Sisters' had arrived on the scene in November 1854. By the time the war ended, there were more than 300 of them serving in the war zone – many times more than what the British and its allies had on their side. Some of them were also deployed in the field hospitals closer to the war front. In recognition of their services, the Russian government had even instituted and awarded medals to them. [7] And yet, for a variety of reasons beyond the scope of this narration, the Russians failed to exploit the advantages of so promising a start to reforming their military nursing services.

Unlike the British army which had female nurses in their base hospitals since the 1850s, Royal Navy (RN) started the process of employing them only in 1884 when ten sisters under a matron were appointed to one of the naval hospitals. However, they were not subject to naval discipline and their status remained as civilians attached to the navy.[8] Later, when Queen Alexandra's Imperial Nursing Service (QAIMNS) was formed in 1902, all the nurses serving in the army and the navy became part of the regular force.

Women as nurses were unobtrusively tiptoeing into the profession of arms in other countries too. For example, Military Health Service in France had established two training schools for women nurses by 1890 for in-take in the army. Similarly, the Surgeon General in the USA realized the importance of female nurses for better soldier care and prevailed upon the US Congress in 1901 to sanction the formation of the United States Army Nursing Corps (USANC). Thus started the recruitment of trained and registered female nurses in the US army.

As to the Indian scene is concerned, the evolution of military nursing in India generally followed the British pattern and timeline. It was in 1867 that the training of nurses started in India at St Stephen's Hospital in Delhi; though not for the army per se. The first batch of British Army nurses arrived in India in 1888 and was assigned to some of the military hospitals. That set-in motion the commencement of the nursing service in the Indian Army. Slowly their numbers grew and the Indian Army Nursing Service came into being in 1893. It then became part of QAIMNS in 1902. When First World War (WW-I) broke out in 1914 there were just about 300 British nurses in India. To meet the sudden spurt in the demand for nurses in various theatres of war, the Indian Nursing Service was established as an adjunct to the QAIMNS. With that, for the first time, trained Indian nurses started getting enrolled in the army.

Conclusion

Evidently, it was the nursing services that led to women's entry into the profession of arms. Quiet and sans fanfare it was almost like an entry by invitation since women nurses were welcomed and readily accepted by men into their exclusive preserve for the difference they made by their quiet demeanor and caring presence. Much in the manner of the quote at the beginning of this chapter, women had shaken the very basics of military thinking with their gentle ways.

By the time WW-I broke out there were women in the military nursing services of all the modern armies and navies of the world – air force had not arrived on the scene till then. However, women were destined to play a far greater role in WW-I, and an even bigger one in World War II (WW-II), as the next chapter brings out.

Endnotes

1. During their colonial rule the British continued with the practice in India and the system of *'Regimental Baniya'* continues in the Indian Army even today.

2. Andrew de la Garza, *Mughals at War: Babur, Akbar and the Indian Military Revolution, 1500 - 1605,* The Ohio State University, USA, 2010, PP 243. (https://etd.ohiolink.edu/apexprod/rws_etd/send_file/send?accession=osu1 274894811&disposition=inline) Accessed on July 23, 2021.

3. Philip Mason, *A Matter of Honour,* EBD Educational Private Limited, Dehradun, India, 1988, pp 223.

4. M. C. Devilbiss, *Women and Military Service: A History, Analysis, and Overview of Key Issues,* Air University Press, Maxwell Air Force Base, Alabama USA, 1990, pp 1.

5. Reporting for *The Times* for close to two years he became the first 'war correspondent'.

6. D Collette Wadge (Ed), *Women in Uniform,* Sampson Low, Marston and Co, Ltd, 1946, pp 4.

7. For more details see https://rn-journal.com/journal-of-nursing/russian-nurses-after-the-crimean-war (Accessed on July 28, 2021).

8. See note 6, pp 1.

CHAPTER - 4

"CRACKING THE GLASS CEILING": WOMEN IN UNIFORM IN THE TWO WORLD WARS

"Women were everywhere, stirred to heroic deeds in this epic time."

William George Fitzgerald

(A British writer, and journalist who wrote under the pseudonym Ignatius Phayre)

The Setting

During the first six months of 1914, a group of high-minded Englishmen was making plans to celebrate in the following year, an important centenary: 18 June 1915 would be the hundredth anniversary of the Battle of Waterloo.¹ Regrettably, all their plans came to naught when the First World War burst upon the scene on June 14, 1914.

For a variety of good reasons WW-I was also referred to as 'The Great War'. It had all the European empires at war and had also drawn USA and Japan into it. Vastly improved rail and road transportation systems had allowed both the warring sides to field and sustain armies larger than ever before. With improved communication systems, such as telegraph and telephones at their disposal, commanders could exercise far better command and control over their forces. It surely was a modern war that saw the arrival of tanks, submarines, and aircraft in the battle spaces of land, sea, and air. It also experienced the use of flame throwers and poisonous gases. Collectively they all made it a deadly war. Within two months of its outbreak, British writer Herbert George Wells had penned an article titled 'The War That Will End War'. ² The heading clearly indicated how he viewed the outcome of the war. Though The Great War failed to live up to any such expectations, in the contextual framework of this chapter, it did usher in a notable change – that of greater participation of uniformed women in the war zone.

The change was in fact triggered by the unprecedented number of casualties suffered by the warring sides. By the time the war ended with the signing of the Armistice in November 1918, an estimated 9 to 11 million military personnel had been killed, and even more, were wounded – some maimed for life – and some more were reported as 'Missing presumed dead'. Needless to say, armies started facing manpower shortages as the war progressed. The situation became critical during the battle of Somme – July to November 1916 – which alone accounted for a million dead and wounded. Able-bodied men were required to replace the casualties on the frontline and a practical solution had to be found post haste. "Before August 1914, neither military nor civil authorities in Britain had given serious thought to the question of how women might best be organized if war broke out." ³ There were few takers of the idea that women could face hazards of military service even in a supporting role. Initially, women's contribution to the war effort was only as nurses. Nevertheless, the War Office soon realized that a sizeable number of troops were nowhere near the sound of booming guns, or the staccato of the machine-gun fire, and were engaged in duties that could well be performed by women. That set the ball rolling.

Women in WW-I

To start with many more nurses were enrolled by the British – as also by other warring nations – to cater to the high rate of casualties. QAIMNS for example had only about 300 nurses on its roll in 1914 but their number rose to over 10,000 by the time the war ended. The British Expeditionary Force eventually had a total of 23,000 nurses while the French Army had 63,000 of them. Germans on the opposite side had as many as 91,000 nurses and women volunteers. Indeed, "One of the staples of Great War propaganda was the poster showing a nurse (always beautiful and composed, always immaculate) bending over a handsome young soldier (calm and alert, seriously but not mortally wounded, never injured in ways unpleasant to the eye) who gazes up at her in gratitude and admiration." [4]

Be that as it may, soon 'First Aid Nursing Yeomanry' (FANY), a mounted corps, also swung into action. These women risked their lives as ambulance drivers in Belgium and in France. Later, FANY also ran convoys to repatriate prisoners of war (POW). 'Women's Army Auxiliary Corps' (WAAC) and 'Women's Royal Navy Service' (WRNS) came into being in 1917 to free soldiers and sailors from non-combatant duties. 'Women's Royal Air Force' (WRAF) was established only towards the end of the war in 1918. Divided into many branches, these women served as drivers, messengers, mechanics, clerical staff, radio operators, and cryptographers. A total of 100,000 English women joined the armed forces during the war. While most served at home, about 9000 of them also served beyond home shores in France and Belgium. "They did so only because they chose to: under the impulse of patriotism, or monetary incentives, or the hope of improving the status of their sex." [5] Lest it is lost sight of it must also be mentioned that a large number of working-class women contributed to the war effort by working in the ammunition factories. Handling explosives and chemicals for long working hours tended to give their skin a yellow tinge and were fondly nicknamed 'Canaries'. In the absence of adequate protective gears, many of them died due to overexposure to the explosive they handled – trinitrotoluene or TNT.

When the British declared war, de facto, all colonies and dominions of the Empire were also at war, and women from these countries also contributed their might – essentially as nurses – to the war effort. For example, nurses from Australia served in Egypt, Gallipoli, and France. Similarly, the Canadian Nursing Service "Conducted itself in the First World War with great gallantry on all fronts, and a memorial to its work stands in the Hall of Fame in the Canadian parliamentary buildings." [6]

Americans entered the war only towards the middle of 1917. Wiser by the happenings on the war front, they were better prepared for the war with clearer ideas about women's participation. Their army and navy nurse corps had over 22,000 female nurses catering to their war-wounded on the battlefield and on the hospital ships. Some were also deployed to look after the sick and the wounded in the POW camps. Before entering the war, the Americans had also formed the 'Female Telephone Operators Unit' as part of its Army Signal Corps. It had more than four hundred switchboard operators who were usually referred to as 'Hello Girls'. Most of them were proficient in both English and French. However, it was US Navy that first enlisted women into the regular armed forces. Over 11,000 of them joined the US Navy during the war doing shore jobs to free sailors for active duty on the high seas. U.S. Marine Corps soon followed suit and had a cadre of some three hundred Women Marine Reservists manning their communications and working as clerical staff.

Whereas no British or American woman took place in the firing line, the Russian women did. With their daring deeds during The Great War, they made far greater inroads in the field of soldiering than the women of all other warring nations. Even as nurses they had tended to their wounded closer to the front – at times also under fire. Unlike all other warring nations of WW-I, Russian women had also erased the boundaries of gendered roles by stepping forward to enlist as regular soldiers in 'Women's Battalions'. These units were disbanded soon after the Russian Revolution in 1917. Though these female soldiers had acquitted themselves creditably in all trials of combat, they failed to get the recognition they deserved from the post-revolution Russian leadership. who preferred to treat the war merely as a 'bourgeois imperialist venture'. [7]

As a point of interest, it is well worth recording that Milunka Savic of Serbia became the most decorated female soldier of the Great War – the only woman to receive the French *Croix de Guerre With The Gold Palm*, twice the French *Légion d'Honneur*, British medal of the *Most Distinguished Order of St Michael*, Russian *Cross of St. George* and of course her own country's *Miloš Obilić* – and she remains so even today.

This brief on the women's role in WW-I will be incomplete without a mention of two of their other courageous engagements serving the war efforts – as spies and as war correspondents. Though not strictly within the ambit of the profession of arms per se, both these activities entailed living dangerously in the war zone – for the spies, it also meant living amongst the enemy. Not to clutter the text with too many details, only two of their exploits, one on each count, is being cited here. The first one is about a spy named Mata Hari. [8] She was a Dutch woman and was perhaps the most famous spy of the war. As an exotic dancer and a stripper, she had many admirers. Some of them could not keep mum, and she was not dumb. When her cover was blown, she was tried by the French on charges of spying for the Germans and was executed by the firing squad. She is said to have refused a blindfold and reportedly also blew a kiss towards the firing squad as they took aim. The second example relates to an English reporter named Dorothy Lawrence. Dressed as a male soldier she reported from the front-line trenches. Because of her failing health, her stint turned out to be rather short. Even so, she must be remembered for her gutsy professional zeal and for setting a trend.

Guns fell silent and The Great War came to an end when the Armistice was signed at eleven o' clock on the eleventh day of the eleventh month of 1918. That day, in a letter to his mother, Albert Einstein wrote "The present leadership seems thoroughly equal to its task." [9] Quite contrary to his belief, the Armistice and the resulting 'Treaty of Versailles', only paved the way for WW-II.

Women in WW-II

If WW-I was "The Great War', the Second World War (1939-1945) went on to eclipse it on all counts of comparison. Its theatres of war stretched from plains of Europe to the deserts of North Africa, and from the teaming jungles of Burma (now Myanmar) to the war in the Pacific. It was also fought for a longer duration. While there was blitzkrieg by the mechanized forces on the ground, carrier-based naval forces projected power on the high seas and the air forces ruled the skies. It accounted for an estimated 21- 25 million dead and wounded military personnel, and twice as many civilian casualties. It was a total war where the strategic bombings by both sides severely punished civilian targets to terrorize and cripple opponents into submission. Technological advancements during the war led to the dropping of the first-ever atomic bomb on Hiroshima. The death and destruction it caused were thus described by a lucky survivor "By evening the fire began to die down and then it went out. There was nothing left to burn. Hiroshima had ceased to exist." [10] The war came to an end when the second one was dropped on Nagasaki. More importantly, and in the context of this write-up, WW-II witnessed greater participation of women in the war.

Besides the traditional role as nurses, and some other tried and tested trades of the First World War, women confidently took on many other combat duties – quite a few right in the battle zones – during the Second World War. To give the readers a fair idea of their commendable contributions, the following text selectively brings on record some of the fields of their telling presence.

In 1940-41, the Germans commenced their bombing campaign targeting British industrial hubs, ports, railways and cities. As one of the measures to counter it, the British brought the Auxiliary Territorial Service (ATS) – an erstwhile voluntary women's organization – under the Army Act and gave its women cadres same status as the serving men. These women were then incorporated in the anti-aircraft units of the Royal Artillery where they took on the duties as spotters, radar operators and as anti-aircraft gun crews. Soon, the rank and file of the ATS were also integrated into the Search Light units. During the night air raids, they picked up and tracked the German bombers with their searchlights helping the anti-aircraft gunners to aim and shoot. As many as 389 of these brave women died while on active duty. It is noteworthy that " Famous members of the ATS included Mary Churchill, youngest daughter of the Prime Minister, Winston Churchill, and Princess (later Queen) Elizabeth, eldest daughter of the King, who trained as a lorry driver and mechanic." [11]

USA entered WW-II only after the Japanese attacked Pearl Harbour in December 1941. Soon enough American forces were heavily committed in all the theatres of war and with them were the

American women in uniform. Close to 350,000 US women served in various capacities in the US armed forces. Their lady doctors and nurses set enviable professional standards by attending to the casualties almost on the front line. For example, within four hours of the Normandy landings, they were already on the beaches still bristling with enemy fire. Not surprisingly, during the war, sixteen of them died due to enemy actions, 68 were taken as PsOW, and close to a thousand of them were decorated for their bravery and distinguished services. American women had also made great inroads in the technical fields – as surgical and X-ray technicians, electrical and instrument specialists, flight mechanics, signal equipment repairers, expert air photo interpreters, and so on. Some were even regular pilots testing repaired planes at the airbases.

Russians had an estimated 800,000 women serving in their armed forces and, as in the First World War, quite a few of them were also in actual combat. They were integrated in the fighting units as tank crews, machine gunners and as snipers. It may be interesting to note that one of their highly decorated snipers, Roza Shanina, was credited with 59 confirmed kills. Russians were also the first ones to allow women pilots to fly combat missions. One of their Night Bomber Regiment, 'The Night Witches', was an all-women unit – pilots, navigators, flight engineers, and the ground support staff. Russian women pilots flew some 30,000 missions during the war.

It would be unfair not to recall the sacrifices of women who, without donning the uniform, verily courted extreme danger as part of the resistance movement in all the German occupied territories. They countered and degraded the activities of the invaders in every possible way – providing safe houses to the guerrillas, saboteurs, and intelligence agents, temporarily sheltering the escaping POW and crashed pilots, hiding persecuted Jews, surreptitiously carrying out anti-Nazi propaganda, acting as messengers and so on. If caught they faced torture and possible execution. Many of them did.

Lastly, a word about the Indian women's contribution towards the war efforts. Admittedly, strict social norms of a deeply conservative India had prevented them from being part of the First World War, but they more than made up their absence in the Second one. In

January 1942 Indian lady doctors started joining the Indian Medical Service as commissioned officers. The formation of the Women's Auxiliary Corps (WAC) a little later that year also gave Indian women an opportunity to be part of the war cause. It was a rare 'first' for them. Their numbers swelled to a little over 8,000 during the war and were part of the Indian Army wherever it served. Some more women joined in when the Naval Wing of the WAC was established in 1944. In accordance with British policy, they all served in various capacities in non-combat roles. Addressing the WAC parade in Delhi in November 1944, General Sir Claude Auchinleck, the then Commander in Chief, India, said, "You are definitely helping to win the war." [12]

It may be recalled that, while helping the British to win the war, a section of the Indian women had also taken up arms against them. Exploits of 'Rani of Jhansi Regiment' of the INA have already been covered in an earlier chapter.

Any account of Indian women in WW-II would be incomplete without a mention of one of the most famous spies of the war – Noor Inayat Khan, a descendent of the ruling family of Mysore that had settled down in France. She was fluent both in English and in French. The family shifted to England when the Germans occupied France. It is there that she took to spying for the British in France under the cover name Madeleine. She was captured by the Germans in October 1943 while relaying information to the British. Though tortured she divulged no details about her handlers or her activities. She made an unsuccessful escape attempt after which she was labeled as 'Highly Dangerous' and was shifted to Dachau concentration camp where, on September 13, 1944, she was executed. She was posthumously awarded George Cross by the British and *Croix de Guerre with a Silver Star* by the French government. Much later, on November 28, 2018, New York Times also published an obituary honouring her heroic acts and sacrifices.

Conclusion

During the difficult times of the two world wars, hundreds and thousands of women of all the warring countries had voluntarily stepped forward to take up a range of soldierly duties – quite a few of them in actual combat – breaking all established social norms and surpassing all previous war experiences. Their sense of elation was best conveyed by a French girl who, at the time of her enrolment, had said "For the first time I was going to be someone. I would count in the world." [13] No job supporting the war cause was high or low for those motivated women. Throughout the war they had excelled in their assigned duties and had demonstrated that they could do a man's work as efficiently if not better. Even in the combat roles they had come out with flying colours.

After WW-I, the conformists had tended to view the influx of women in the war zone only as a temporary measure to tide over the crisis – more in the nature of a flock of migratory birds – and expected them to go back and settle down in their customary family roles. In fact, in a letter to an English daily, one such gentleman even complained of women "making themselves and, what is more important, the King's uniform, ridiculous." [14] However, by the time the Second World War ended there were no more doubts about the permanency of women's significant presence in the profession of arms. They had stepped out of their socially discriminatory grooves and were there to stay. It was a eureka moment of self-realization for women. They had cracked the glass ceiling.

It is not that women have taken to arms only in support of the state. Quite often they have done so against the state too. The next chapter deals with the subject matter.

Endnotes

1. Trevor Wilson, *The Myriad Faces of War,* Polity Press Cambridge, in Association with Basil Blackwell, Oxford, 1988, pp 7.

2. British newspaper, *The Daily News,* August 14, 1914.

3. Margaret Randolph Hingonnet, Jane Jenson, Sonya Michel, Margaret Collins Weitz (Ed), *Behind the Lines : Gender and the Two World Wars,* Yale University Press, New Haven and London, 1987, PP 114..

4. G J Meyer, *A World Undone : The Story of the Great War, 1914-1918,* Bantam Dell New York, 2006, pp 576.

5. See Note 1, pp 705.

6. D Collette Wadge (Ed), *Women in Uniform,* Sampson Low, Martson and Co, Ltd, 1946, pp 248.

7. For details see https://encyclopedia.1914-1918-online.net/article/womens_mobilization_for_war_russian_empire (Accessed on August 19, 2021)

8. Mata Hari means"The Light of Day" in Malay. Her real name was Margaretha Geertruida Zelle McLeod.

9. Martin Gilbert, *First World War,* Weidenfeld and Nicolson, London, 1994, pp 505.

10. *Eye Witness History of World War - II, Volume 4 : Victory,* Gallery Edition, Bantam Books, New York, 1962, pp 204.

11. See https://en.wikipedia.org/wiki/Auxiliary_Territorial_Service. (Accessed on August 27, 2021)

12. Professor R S Kaushala, *Women Warriors : Brave Deeds Done by Women in 2 Great Wars,* The Standard Publishing Co, Ambala City, India, First Edition ,1944, pp 63.

13. See Note 4, pp 577.

14. Ibid, pp 579.

CHAPTER - 5

"THE CRACKED GLASS CEILING": ABOUT WOMEN BEARING ARMS AGAINST THE STATE

"Rebels and non-conformists are often the pioneers and designers of change."

- Indira Gandhi

Opening Remarks

It may be recalled that all through the ages, women have been kept away from actual combat. And yet, as the earlier chapters reveal, there have been illustrious warring queens and she-soldiers in the era gone by. They had soldiered on either motivated by their sense of duty, or the force of circumstances or by their ambitions – queens defending or expanding their kingdoms, for example. Some had even fought on disguised as men for their personal reasons. In the more recent past, from their rather limited participation in the wars of the late nineteenth century, women had made an emphatic entry into the armed forces during the two world wars. It may be noted that all examples of the women soldiers of the yore, or of the ones of the twentieth century mentioned erenow, relate to those who had taken to arms in support of their rulers or the governments.

It is equally true that both the past and the present history are replete with instances where women have also been part of the armed struggles against the state – not only as covert supporters and facilitators without weapons but also as hardcore members of the violent military wings. Developed societies tend to view women's participation in such political violence as unusual. Nevertheless, such occurrences do raise very many complex questions. Such as, what motivates these women to join insurgent cadres, terrorist organizations, or non-state armed groups? Is it their conviction or are they brainwashed into it? Or is it that they are forcefully nudged and mobilized by the hardline recruiters of the movement? Do they take to violence only to support the stated goal(s) of the movement, or do some also get drawn into it to settle scores of the atrocities suffered – a rape victim for example? What happens to them once the movement peters out or fails? Are they rehabilitated? Does a stigma remain attached to them? What is society's attitude towards these combatant women once they lay down their arms?

This write-up steers clear of the aforesaid weighty issues and reflects on women who, despite the hazards and the pitfalls of such undertakings, find compelling reasons and motivations to join these violent ventures. What's more, all anti-national elements also prefer to have women cadres amongst them for a variety of good reasons. For example, their presence tends to give a degree of inclusive and appealing legitimacy to the 'cause' of their violent protest. Women also enjoy some intrinsic advantages over their male counterparts in such clandestine movements – seemingly harmless, they arouse lesser suspicion and alarm amidst the security forces and stand better chances of success in their secret missions. Their actions also have greater propaganda value. In short, their inclusion is a desirable and practical option for violent groups. Not surprisingly, therefore, and quite contrary to the general perception, women have been, and continue to be, part of extremist organizations in large numbers championing diverse causes in very many countries across the globe. More about their exploits a little later.

Low-intensity conflicts are quite different from conventional wars. Therefore, for a better understanding of the text that follows, a brief and simple explanation of some of the terms related to such armed struggles is attached as Appendix C. It is also clarified that the terms 'insurgents', 'guerillas', 'terrorists', and 'extremists' have been used interchangeably in this chapter.

Olden Times

It appears that in olden times an insurgency or a proxy war was not viewed or defined in the manner it is now. It was usual for the then historians to record such armed struggles as uprising, rebellion, mutiny, disorder, or simply as banditry. For example, consequent to Alexander's conquest of Egypt in 332 BCE his trusted lieutenants ruled Egypt wisely and tried to assimilate the Egyptians. Yet they were considered 'outsiders'. The unease erupted into an armed uprising that lasted for twenty long years from 205 BCE to 186 BCE. Though it had all the elements of an insurgency, historical records show it as 'The Great Egyptian Revolt'. Similarly, Judaea – located in the southern part of present-day Israel – came under the Romans in 40 BCE. Their efforts to 'Romanize' the society did not go down well with the native Jews. The tensions led to the Jewish Independence Movement in 6 CE. Small armed bands of Jews took on the might of the Roman legions for six long decades before they were surrounded in Jerusalem. "Eventually, it was announced that the last stubborn insurgents would receive no quarter, and the subsequent Roman breakthrough saw them slaughtered to a man." [1] Despite all the trappings of an insurgency this too is referred to as 'The Jewish Revolt'. Aforesaid instances of insurgencies apart, one can even find an example of a proxy war in the ancient world. In the eighth century BCE when the all-powerful Assyrians were expanding their empire, some of the smaller states smarting under the defeat had taken the recourse of – what will pass for a proxy war now – inciting and covertly supporting a stronger one against the Assyrians.

What is important in the context of this chapter is the fact that women were not part of any such conflicts in the past. By and large, they were not there in such struggles even till the eighteenth-century CE. As an exception, Claire Lacombe of France provides one of the rare examples. In 1792 she joined an extremist group of the French Revolution. Known as 'Red Rosa' in her group she was a fearless fighter. Once she was even wounded in action, however, she was soon captured and jailed.

Such cases remained isolated even in the nineteenth century. In 1813 Columbia, Maria Antonia Santos Plata is known to have raised and led rebel guerrillas [2] against the Spanish colonizers. In France, women insurgents were actively involved in more ways than one in the July revolution of 1830 and again in the Paris uprising of 1848 – Augustine Péan even suffered injuries while manning her barricade. Though few and far apart, there were some such cases of women insurgents in the second half of that century too. The early twentieth century also witnessed a few such cases. For example, in 1906, Qui Jin of China had raised and led young revolutionaries against the then corrupt government in office. She is often referred to as the 'Chinese Joan of Arc'. Similarly, in 1911 in far-off Mexico, Margarita Neri led an armed band of followers against the dictatorial regime of President Diaz. She and her fellow fighters were known for their ferocity. Just for the records, both these female insurgent leaders were executed when captured

Recent Past to the Present

Evidently, over a period of time, women had steadily graduated from being mere bystanders to sympathizers and then from being supporters to fighters. The frequency of their active participation in greater numbers is a more recent phenomenon. Starting around the mid-twentieth century, it became a usual occurrence with the impulses of the two main global events acting as the catalyst – the process of balkanization in the post WW-II era and the shrinking of the colonial rule. These two led to the emergence of a number of new countries striving for the political consolidation of their new dominions. For differing reasons, many of them faced serious internal troubles leading to prolonged low-intensity conflicts which in turn saw increasing participation of women combatants. Data collected by the researchers show that, towards the turn of the twentieth century, women were actively involved in the internal armed conflicts of as many as thirty-eight countries and that their numbers varied between one-tenth and one-third of the total armed cadres. It is noteworthy that jihadist movements have been more orthodox in allowing women to take part in these conflicts. Be that as it may, not to clutter the text, accounts of only a select few examples of women combatants are being narrated to give a summative overview of women extremists who, driven by their own callings, had/have taken to violence against the state.

Women Insurgents

Liberation Tigers of Tamil Eelam (LTTE), spearheading the Tamil separatist movement in Sri Lanka, was a fearsome armed group. Besides the ground troops, it also had naval and air wings with a strong presence of women cadres. Having joined the LTTE, all women recruit had to pick a new name – *Nom de guerre* – for themselves. It then became their organizational identity. "In the Tamil movement, women initially performed paramilitary and support roles but were used in combat after 1985. - - - - Of the estimated total cadre strength of 10,000 to 15,000, women account for nearly one-third, and - - - - there is no discrimination based on sex when it comes to training and combat operations." [3]

Saroja (not her real name), a diehard female soldier of LTTE's all-women unit had participated in the battle of Elephant Pass leading to Jaffna in 2000. During the attack, she was hit by a splinter and also suffered two gunshot wounds. Later, in her testimony, she vividly narrated her experiences with the LTTE – strict camp life, harsh training schedules, elaborate operational preparations *et al.* [4] Referring to Norway brokered Cease Fire Agreement (CFA) of 2002, she says "When I look back, I think the CFA destroyed the LTTE. - - - - The LTTE became very relaxed. - - - - Desertions shot up. Like me, many left the camp never to return to the LTTE." [5] Unlike Saroja however, there were many others who continued to fight on till the Tigers were finally wiped out, and their elusive chief Prabhakaran was killed, in May 2009.

Naxal movement is an ongoing struggle by the aggrieved sections of the society against the ruling dispensation in many states of central India. Essential details in Appendix C provide the backdrop. By 1980 "Peoples War Group emerged as the most formidable Naxalite formation in the country." [6] Various factions merged in 2004 to form the Communist Party of India (Maoist), (CPI (M)). That has given the Naxal movement greater organizational strength and cohesion.

Its military wing has raised the People's Liberation Guerrilla Army (PLGA) and it has women fighters. "The women cadre is involved in the Maoist struggle at par with its male counterparts. About 40 percent of the Maoist cadre comprises women. They take part in attacks on security forces and other operations as much as male rebels." [7]

In the ongoing proxy war in J&K, women have not taken to the acts of violence but support it nevertheless. Some of them – especially those from the households that have, or had, extremist male member(s) – aggrandize and instill jihadist values in their impressionable young ones. Some others support the 'cause' by joining active women's organizations. "The Dukhataran-i-Millat (Daughters of Faith) and the Khawateen Markaz (Council of Muslim Women) are based on the principles of spreading the correct message of the Quran, on the role of women in Islam and the politics of Jihad and revenge." [8]

United Liberation Front of Assam (ULFA) has been active in India's northeastern state of Assam since its inception in 1979 to 'liberate' Assam and establish an independent sovereign state. The rank and file of ULFA have a select lot of female fighters on its roll. Its well-structured Military Wing also boasts of a 'Volcano Unit' that specializes in target killings and assassinations. "In military operations, particularly the Volcano Unit, took women cadres along as it helped them to avoid police and military search." [9]

In another northeastern state of Manipur, agitations by the separatist faction started in 1977 and had turned violent by 1980. The military wing of the insurgents, the People's Liberation Army, had women in its cadre from the very inception. Some of them had travelled to Kachin in upper Myanmar for their training. These women ultras were "Obviously taking part in combat by the 1990s. This was confirmed when two PLA women were shot dead in an army ambush in the Chandel district of Manipur - - - -." [10]

The trend of armed women in such outfits is not peculiar to India or its immediate neighbourhood. It is prevalent in the troubled spots of the Middle East and so also in the African states.

Latin America is no exception either. "In Nicaragua, women were some 30 percent of soldiers and leaders of the Sandinista National Liberation Front." [11] What is more disturbing is the fact that most of these extremist organizations not only have she fighters but also women suicide bombers.

Female Suicide Bombers

Nobody had imagined that the Kamikaze attacks by the Japanese pilots during the Second World War – an irrational idea of 'a manned missile' – would lead to suicide attacks by human bombs in the not-too-distant future. Regrettably, however, that is precisely what happened when, in December 1981, a Shi'a Islamist drove and blew up his explosive-laden car targeting the Iraqi embassy in Beirut, Lebanon. The idea behind the brutal act was not only to cause death and destruction but also to terrorize political masters and the public alike. The act also posed new challenges for the security forces. Within a few years the option of suicide attacks, and the practice of using female suicide bombers, had become an article of faith for all the extremist organizations across the globe – from Sri Lanka to Chechnya and from the Gaza Strip and Iraq to Nigeria.

Conceding that the purists may have difficulty in accepting suicide bombing under the head 'profession of arms', their acts of violence are against the state nevertheless. Succeeding paragraphs narrate a select few details of some of these deadly outfits and the equally deadly acts of their women cadres: -

> ➤ 'Black Tigers', LTTE's elite group that carried out suicide attacks, also had women in its roll. It was one such female suicide bomber who blew herself up to assassinate Shri Rajeev Gandhi, the Indian Prime Minister, in May 1991. Her 'stand by' was also a female Black Tiger. Similarly, in April 2006, it was again a woman suicide bomber who had attacked Lieutenant General Sarath Fonseka, the then Chief of the Sri Lankan army. [12] Of the total 'Black Tigers' who died executing their missions, 74 were women.

➢ Hamas, the Palestinian Islamic Militant Organization, has been engaged in an armed struggle against Israel since the late 1980s. Initially, its military wing had reservations about enrolling women fighters. By 2004 it had shed all such inhibitions and had even women suicide bombers amongst them. Nine of them have already blown themselves up attacking various Israeli targets. One of them "Fatma Omar al-Najar, a 57-year-old grandmother with over 30 grandchildren, also detonated herself." [13] The Arab and the Muslim media have been projecting them as martyrs and heroines.

➢ The term 'Black Widows' – *Shahidka* in Russian – refers to Chechnya's female suicide bombers. In existence since the turn of the century, they soon became the weapon of choice for the Chechen rebels. The first female bomber had blown herself up in 2001 to kill a Russian officer to avenge her husband's killing. However, the Black Widows gained worldwide attention only after a series of deadly attacks on varied targets in Moscow – a theatre, an underground train, an open-air concert, a busy car park, and so on – between 2004-2006. Their involvement in the crash of two Russian passenger aircraft has always been suspected though never established.

Foregoing details represent only the tip of the iceberg since "---- between 1986 and 2005, female bombers committed more than 200 suicide attacks." [14] The trend continued and others soon followed suit. For example, suicide attacks by Iraqi women steadily increased after 2007. From 2014 onwards Boko Haram, the violent separatist group based in northern Nigeria, has also been engaged in this inhuman activity. Similarly, facing serious military reverses towards mid-2017, the Islamic State of Iraq and Syria (ISIS) resorted to using women for such attacks. In July alone that year, there were twenty such incidents. Admittedly, while some of these female carriers of death may have been coerced or tricked into these gruesome acts by their wily handlers, surely there were many more who had done so willingly.

As an aside, a mention must be made of an interesting and out-of-the-ordinary example of Phoolan Devi, the Indian 'Bandit Queen' who had gate-crashed into the men's world of armed banditry. She was an abused woman and a rape victim who became a ruthless female dacoit. She is known for the Behmai Massacre of 1981 where her gang shot dead 22 men of the village in a revenge killing. She surrendered two years later and was tried. However, all charges against her were later withdrawn and, in due course, she got elected as a Member of the Parliament twice. She was assassinated in 2001. Whereas her armed exploits were not against the state, they certainly were a law-and-order problem for the state.

To Conclude

"Over the last two decades, civil conflicts have more than doubled, jumping from 30 in 2001 to 70 in 2016." [15] Justification or otherwise of all such conflicts notwithstanding, the fact remains that with their unprecedented participation in these armed struggles, women have cracked the glass ceiling to step into the men's preserve of bearing arms. Women who join such banned outfits are strong in their bodies, mind, and of their convictions. Some die championing the 'cause' while some disillusioned ones give up and surrender. The ones who are persevering are making their mark amongst the hordes of rough men and their acts of violence.

"Rebel leaders started recruiting and using women operators in underground militant operations when they were still off the radar of those in the business of counter-terrorism." [16] Nevertheless, just as an increasing number of female insurgents, rebels, and extremists have taken up arms against the state, many more women across the globe have done so in support of the state. The next chapter dwells on the subject with an Indo-centric pitch.

Endnotes

1. Emerson T. Brooking, *ROMA SURRECTA: Portrait of a Counterinsurgent Power, 216 BC - AD 72,* College Undergraduate Research Electronic Journal, 5-2011, University of Pennsylvania, USA, pp 93.

2. The Spanish word, a diminutive of *Guerra,* meaning 'a small war' got introduced during the Peninsular War, 1808-1814.

3. For details see Tsjeard Bouta, Georg Frerks, Ian Bannon, *Gender, Conflict and Development,* The World Bank, Washington DC, USA, 2005, Box 2.1, pp 13.

4. For details see M R Narayan Swami, *The Tiger Vanquished : LTTE's Story,* SAGE Publications India Pvt Ltd, New Delhi, India, 2010, pp lxxiii- lxxvi

5. Ibid, pp lxxvii.

6. V R Raghavan, *The Naxal Threat : Causes, State Responses and Consequences,* Vij Books Pvt Ltd, New Delhi, India, 2011, pp 103

7. Rahul Pandita, *Hello Bastar : The Untold Story of India's Maoist Movement,* Tranquebar Press, New Delhi, India, 2011, pp 97.

8. Anuradha M Chenoy, *Militarism & Women in South Asia,* Kali for Women, New Delhi, India, 2002, pp 153.

9. Arpita Anant (ed), *Non-State Armed Groups In South Asia : A Preliminary Structured Focused Comparison,* Pentagon Security International, New Delhi, India, 2012, pp 111.

10. Rasmi Saksena, *She Goes to War : Women Militants of India,* Speaking Tiger Publishing, Pvt Ltd, New Delhi, India, 2018, pp 184.

11. See Note 3 above, pp11.

12. Though severely wounded the General survived the attack and led his army to finally decimate LTTE in 2009. He rose to be a Field Marshal.

13. Yoram Schweitzer, *Palestinian Female Suicide Bombers: Virtuous Heroines or Damaged Goods?,* Originally published in the *Anthology: Female Terrorism and Militancy: Agency, Utility, and Organization.* Ness, Cindy (ed). Routledge, February 2008, pp 2.

14. Kathleen Turner, *The Rise of Female Suicide Bombers,* Counter Terrorist Trends and Analysis, Vol 8, Issue 3, Mar 2018, pp 15.

15. Paula San Pedro, *Oxfam Intermón Report Number 51,* March 2019, pp 2.

16. See Note 9 above, pp xv.

CHAPTER - 6

"THE CRUMBLING GLASS CEILING": ABOUT WOMEN BEARING ARMS FOR THE STATE

"The question is not who is going to let me; It is who is going to stop me."

Alice O'Connor
(Better known by her pen name Ayn Rand.)

The Necessity of Security Forces Other Than Militaries

All internal conflicts have different motivations – separatist ideology, the struggle for socio-economic fulfillment, ethnic strife, religious fundamentalism, leftist inclinations, rebellion against the dictatorial regime, and so on – and therefore have different roots, goals, agendas, and *modi operandi*. Whereas resolution for all these grey-area conflicts lies in the political domain, each needs to be addressed differently. Since the government's counteractive political initiatives take time to be effective, and cannot materialize amid the troubled setting of the ongoing violent agitations, security forces are deployed to maintain law and order. To that end, all affected nation states raise and maintain suitably trained and equipped forces, other than their militaries, to keep the situation under control and to give a fair chance to the government initiatives to come into their own.

It transpires that India is afflicted by quite a few of these violent upheavals. It is dealing with proxy war in J&K, insurgency in the northeast, and serious Naxal problems in some of the states of central India. To crown it all, India also experiences occasional terror strikes and communal riots. Some of these internal conflicts have strong cross-border linkages necessitating aggressive manning and surveillance of the troubled borders. Even otherwise, all borders need to be managed not only to guard against cross-border terrorism, gun-running, drug trafficking, and illegal migration but also to monitor the regular movement of personnel and goods. That being the case, besides strengthening the police force, India has also raised a number of armed constabularies and para-military forces to effectively deal with the situation. Some of these assist the state governments in maintaining law and order while some others guard our borders. And thereby hangs the tale – that of women gaining entry into all these organizations and taking up arms for the state. They are now rubbing shoulders with their male counterparts to ward off threats from without, and also to quell threats within to restore normalcy.

Whereas women's increasing presence in police and similar other forces is a global phenomenon, the text that follows is Indo-centric. Besides the police, only a select few Indian para-military forces are being covered here. The narration brings out the 'why' and 'how' of the women's entry into these forces and how the central police and para-military forces have coped with these systemic changes. The start is being made from women's enrollment in the civil police.

A Brief on the Origins of Policing and Women in the Police

In ancient times the empire builders had no police forces per se and it was their armies that enforced law and order. In ancient Egypt, local administrators did maintain a body of men to protect government assets and public places. But they had little authority and did nothing more than guarding. Similarly, V*igils* who came into being in Roman Emperor Caesar's time were more in nature of watchmen rather than police. Towards the end of the 15th century Greek word *Polis,* meaning 'city' and the Latin word '*politia*' meaning 'citizenship', gave rise to the French word 'police' implying 'public order'. By the 19th century the use of the word, and the concept of policing, had spread across the globe. All nation-states now maintain police forces to protect people and their properties, prevent and investigate crimes, and maintain law and order. Their powers, including that of arrest, are laid down by the states. To begin with, policing was a male preserve.

By the second half of the 19th century, women in the western world were increasingly stepping out of their homes to seek employment. In the wake of this social phenomenon came increasing crimes against them. With the passage of time, because of the sensitivity attached to the nature of crimes against women, the presence of female constables was considered desirable. The USA was apparently first off the block when Marie Owens joined the Chicago Police force in 1891. Germany enrolled their first woman police in 1903. Sweden followed suit in 1908 at the behest of their National Women's Council. By 1923 Poland had a separate 'Women's Section' in their police department. Though all these women police played an important role in cases related to women and children – in their search and arrest for example – they were seen more as a part of a social welfare measure rather than as police and were assigned softer duties. Consequently, the enrolment of women in the police force remained a slow process and their numbers increased in fits and starts. However, all such perceptions and equations changed with women's forceful participation in the First World War that show-cased their unexplored tough side. It became clear that, if they could face the challenges in the war zone, surely they were capable of going *'mano a mano'* with men in policing too. Consequently, in the post-WW-I era, their numbers increased at a brisker pace.

Women in the Indian Police Service

In India, towards the late 18th century, the British abolished the *Zamindari* system and took over the responsibility of policing from the *Zamindars* – the local landlords whose oft misused fiefdom it had been. After the uprising of 1857, a Police Commission was set up and its recommendations led to the formulation of the Police Act of 1861, which laid the foundation of the present system of policing in India. In due course, Indians were also allowed to appear in the competitive examination to join the force as officers.

During colonial rule, the entry of women into the Indian police followed the British visions and patterns. In England, the British had enrolled their first female police in 1907 as an 'aide' to interrogate and/or record statements of women victims. It was only in 1915 that a woman constable, Edith Smith, was enrolled with powers to arrest like her male counterparts. By the early 1920s, backed by the impulses of WW-I, their enrolment had commenced on a regular basis in England. In the more conservative India however, their entry started only towards the late 1930s to deal with women in law and order situations – to evict or arrest female protesters of the Independence movement for example. At that time "There were also few other examples of women police in other states like Travancore, Gujrat, and Kerala." [1] Indeed, Travancore Royal Police had women constables as early as 1933. Even so, in post-Independence India, the police force was essentially an all-male bastion. Delhi Police was first to commence regular enrolment of female police in 1948. However, it was only in 1972 that the first lady officer, Kiran Bedi, joined the Indian Police Service.

With the passage of time, and with increasing crimes against women, the role of women police has also increased manifold. So have their numbers – from 1,05,325 in 2013 to 1,69,550 in 2017 [2] and to 2,27,889 by 2021. Even so, only 10% of the Indian police are female. [3] Since nearly half the Indian population is females, the current percentage is woefully skewed. Future plans aim not only to have many more 'Women Protection Cell' and 'Women Police Station' but also to have enough women police constables in all police stations so that a' Women's Help Desk' can be manned round the clock.

It may be noted that, as part of the civil police, women are also in the District Armed Reserve and State Armed Police. They are also there in the Traffic Police, Intelligence Branch, and Special Police Units. "Legally there is no distinction between the duties of a policewoman and a policeman. In practice, however, the policewomen are frequently used for certain 'specialized' or selected tasks- - - - -." [4] For example, to arrest, search, escort, and interrogate female offenders. Over the years they have proved themselves as good as men in 'Hard Skills' and even better in 'Soft Skills'. Because of their demeanour, female victims of violent crimes are less hesitant to file their complaints and record statements before them. Public complaints against them for the use of excessive force, or for losing their moral compass, are also few and far apart. Unfortunately, "The contribution made by women in the police force is not so visible because their numbers are so few." [5] Be that as it may, collectively all these enterprising women are doing their best, round the clock, to help the state in ensuring public order.

For actual numbers of women in various units and branches of civil police as of January 1, 2020, see Appendix D.

Assam Rifles (AR)

Assam was annexed by the British in 1826. By 1835 they had raised 'Cachar Levy' – a para-military force – to protect the planters and the tea estates in Assam, and also to maintain law and order in the Lushai Hills (present-day Mizoram). In due course, the force was variously designated before finally becoming Assam rifles in 1917. Nevertheless, all along it has remained an area-specific force with its primary role in the northeast, where they have been "The custodians of law and order, pioneers of every advance into the interiors, the guardians of our borders and, above all, the friends of the hill people." [6] The oldest amongst all the para-military forces in India, AR has grown from five battalions at the time of independence to 46 at present.

The proposal to have women in the force was first mooted in 2012. It took three years of deliberations – to weigh the pros and cons of the concept – and administrative preparations before the proposal was agreed to. Thereafter, the process of women's entry was set in motion by selecting prospective women recruits through all India recruitment rallies. It was in April 2016 that the first batch of hundred women was posted to different units deployed in the troubled northeast to deal with women agitators – to detain, frisk, and interrogate them. They were also incorporated in the 'Road Opening Party' and in the oft-executed 'Cordon and Search Operations'. They have not looked back ever since. These AK-47 wielding Riflewomen of AR in their camouflaged battle gear have not only been up to the mark in their operational missions but were equally impressive in their shining ceremonials as they marched down the Rajpath on January 26, 2019.

In August 2020, a platoon of about thirty women was for the first time deployed at various security checkpoints close to the Line of Control (LoC) in the hostile Kupwara and Tangdhar sectors in J&K. Besides their mission-oriented duties, these women have also been instrumental in bridging the gap with the local women. By early 2021 these gusty Riflewomen were also patrolling the leech-infested teeming jungles of the Indo-Myanmar border to prevent the illegal influx of people, drug trafficking, and smuggling.

In sum, whether in J&K or in the northeast, to check infiltration or to crack down on drug trafficking, to deal with the women agitators, or bridge the gap with the locals, these women have taken to arms to serve the state – without ifs and buts.

Border Security Force (BSF)

Till early 1965, in some sections of the Indo-Pak border, the Border Out Posts (BOPs) were manned by the state armed police. In Apr-May of 1965, there was localized tension along the border with Pakistan in Rann of Kuchh, and some of the BOPs were attacked by the Pak forces. Those manning the BOPs were unable to repulse the attacks. The army had to be called in. Consequently, the necessity of having a more potent force to man the border was felt that "would also enable the Army to keep away from the border even in periods of some degree of tension."[7] Thus, soon after the Indo-Pak conflict of 1965, BSF came into being on December 1, 1965. On the basis of their experiences and the operational requirements, it grew fast in both strength and stature. Water Wing was added in 1966 to effectively patrol creeks and riverine terrains. Air Wing was formed in 1969 for quick movement of troops in times of crisis, the move of med teams in the event of natural calamities, for aerial reconnaissance, move of VIPs, and so on. By 1971 it also had a well-equipped Artillery Wing – the only one amongst the paramilitary forces to have it. With its motto 'Duty unto Death,' the force proudly calls itself 'The First Line of Defence' against encroachments, infiltration bids, smuggling, and trans-border crimes besides of course as the guardians of the border.

Women entry commenced in the BSF as recently as 2008 and the force was applauded for implementing the much-desired change. After some initial hiccups, women's force integration moved at a clipped pace. Here are some datelines: -

- ➤ The First batch of women was deployed along the Indo-Pak border in September 2009.
- ➤ On the occasion of the 48th BSF Day Parade in New Delhi, BSF women's contingent was included in the march past for the first time.
- ➤ In 2016 Tanu Shree Pareek broke through the glass ceiling to become the first woman combat officer in the force. Later, she also had the proud privilege of commanding the Independence Day BSF Parade in 2019 in Srinagar.
- ➤ By March 2021, there were about 30 women in all the BSF battalions deployed along the Rajasthan border.
- ➤ In November 2021, women cadres of BSF were also inducted for guarding the volatile Indo-Pak border in the Jammu sector.
- ➤ Women are now part of all the guards manning the Border Gates.

As of now, there are about 7500 women, including around 140 officers, serving in the BSF – less than 5% of the force – who are bravely roughing it out with their male counterparts to keep a strict vigil along our borders.

Central Industrial Security Force (CISF)

The decade of 1960 signifies the onset of India's industrial revolution. Consequently, it became necessary to have a dedicated force to secure industrial premises and assets. As a result, CISF was raised in 1969. It then grew at a brisk pace and, by an act of parliament, became one of the Central Armed Police Forces (CAPFs) in 1983. The force guards all critical national assets such as nuclear plants, space installations, hydel power projects, steel plants, oil refineries, fertilizer units, airports, seaports, mint, and even monuments like the Taj Mahal. It also transpires that "CISF is the only paramilitary force in India having a highly specialized, trained and fully equipped Fire Wing." [8]

CISF inducted its first batch of women constables in 1987 and the in-take at the officer's level started two years later. They have not looked back ever since and, amongst all the CAPFs maximum number of women are in CISF. It is noteworthy that "Women working in CISF have found working here personally enriching and have integrated themselves with the fabric of the organization in a delightful way." [9]

In the performance of their duties CISF personnel have a maximum public interface with the passengers at the airports and with the commuters at the metro stations. Women cadres have been found to be both assertive and efficient in such public dealings and in diffusing tricky situations. Similarly, "Some of the best instructors in CISF are women, conducting training in diverse areas of specialization ranging from PT, WT, drill, legal matters, accounts, office procedures, aviation security, use of X-BIS, and soft skills". [10] At the Republic Day parade in 2017 CISF women's contingent was adjudged 'The Best Marching Contingent'. Their women officers have excelled as instructors and as staff officers in the UN Peacekeeping missions in Kosovo, Ivory Coast, and South Sudan. Three of their many illustrious sportswomen – Chhaya Adak, Bharti Singh, and Shilpi Singh – are Arjuna awardees. Not surprisingly, in March 2018, a special postage stamp was issued in recognition of CISF women's commendable service to the nation.

Central Reserve Police Force (CRPF)

It came into being as the Crown Representative's Force (CRP) in 1939 and "Its primary duty at the time of its conception was to protect the British residents in sensitive states." [11] It became CRPF post-Independence. As the name suggests, the force is a 'central reserve' to help the state police in times of crisis to maintain law and order, stand by during elections, combat insurgency *et al*. It has grown over the years and is now the largest para-military force in the world. It gives equal opportunity to both male and female applicants to join it.

The increasing involvement of women in crimes, socio-political agitations, and violent anti-national activities – the Naxal movement for example – was *raison d'être* for allowing women's entry into the force. Their presence was particularly desirable on two counts; one, to abide by the laid down regulations for the physical handling of the women trouble makers, and two, thus to shield the force from possible allegations of a misdemeanor in dealing with the women by the male members of the force. Their entry commenced when its first all-woman unit – 88th Mahila Battalion – was raised in February 1986. For the unit, it was baptism by fire since it got operationally committed in the Meerut Riots of 1987, and soon afterwards one of its companies was in action in Sri Lanka as part of the Indian Peace Keeping Force (1987-88) where it was involved in apprehending, frisking and interrogating female LTTE cadres and suspects. The second Mahila Battalion was raised a decade later, followed by four more over the next two decades.

Bastaria Battalion, which was raised in 2018 for operations in the Naxal-infested Bastar region of Chhattisgarh State, has 33% reservation for women in it. In February 2021, thirty-four women from all the six Mahila Battalions were selected to join CRPF's most elite unit – Commando Battalion for Resolute Action (CoBRA) – that specializes in counter-Naxal operations in jungle terrain. Only a month later plans were also afoot to induct women into the 'Valley Quick Reaction Team' operating in J&K. Further, in a first, in September 2021, a select batch of women started its training for VIP security. Incidentally, at the time of writing this, a lady officer, Charu Sinha, is heading CRPF's Srinagar Sector. [12]

All through, and in all their diverse missions, these motivated women have acquitted themselves with distinction – whether as part of the United Nations peacekeeping force in troubled Liberia or as part of the security forces in the Naxals-affected areas in India. Because of their impartial conduct, the question *Quis custodiet ipsos custodes* – a Latin phrase meaning 'Who will guard the guards themselves' – has rarely ever been raised against them. Some of them have died in the line of duty and one of them, Kamlesh Kumra, became the first in the force to be honoured with Ashok Chakra – the highest peacetime gallantry award – on December 1, 2001.

As an aside, it may be interesting to note that CRPF already has an all-woman pipe band and is now in the process of raising an all-woman brass band.

Lest They are Lost Sight of

As mentioned earlier, the foregoing passages have briefly reflected on women's entry, and their accomplishments, in only some of the CAPFs. They have been at the forefront in three other CAPFs too. Indo-Tibetan Border Police (ITBP) has had women not only in their rank and file but also as combat officers since August 2021 and they all get deployed along the disputed border with China. Indeed, "A lot of talk about women in uniform has been about symbolism but the ITBP has taken a bold step by involving women in frontline roles." [13] High-profile National Security Guards (NSG) had inducted a squad of women 'Black Cats' as early as 2011. Admittedly, their numbers have dwindled but efforts are on to revive the squad again. Lastly, Sashastra Seema Bal (SSB) guarding India's borders with Nepal and Bhutan not only has women in the force but also had a lady officer, Archana Ramachandran, as its Chief in 2016-2017 – a first amongst all the CAPFs thus far.

It is noteworthy that women are there in the National Disaster Response Force as 'Disaster Combatants', and 'Rescuers.' Also, the Railway Protection Force has 10% women cadres – maximum in terms of percentage amongst all the aforesaid organizations.

Further, as an aside, it is mentioned that Delhi Police was the first to induct an all-women Anti-Terrorism Squad (ATS) in 2018. At about the same time, Karnataka Police followed suit and started training their first batch of women, 'Garuda Commandos'. In February 2021 Uttarakhand Police also formed a similar all-women ATS with an eye on the then oncoming Maha-Kumbh at Haridwar. [14]

In sum, individually and collectively, all these women have unflinchingly taken to arms to serve the state – to guard our borders, ward off external threats, deal with the upheavals of anti-national threats, and ensure law and order within. For their actual strengths in various CAPFs as of January 1, 2020, see Appendix E.

Conclusion

Just as there are some women who find reasons enough to take up arms against the state, there are many more who have willingly stepped forward to bear arms for the state by joining police services, armed constabularies, and para-military forces. Highly motivated and full of confidence, they have remained unfazed despite the demanding service conditions and the associated professional hazards. Notwithstanding society's deeply ingrained attitude towards them and a degree of bias against them in their own organizations – as 'next to' or 'behind' men – they have faced and overcome unprecedented challenges and have provided enough evidence that in no way are they inferior or less capable than men. With their determined zeal they have broken through the glass ceiling to find their métier.

Having made their mark in the police and the para-military forces, and inspired by Walt Disney's maxim that "It is kind of fun to do the impossible", womenfolk across the globe were ready to chase their dream and confidently took the next step – that of joining the armed forces. The next two chapters dwell on that.

Endnotes

1. Shamim Aleem, *Women in Police Force,* Sterling, New Delhi, 1991, pp 8.

2. Publication by Bureau of Police Research and Development, *Data on Police Organizations, (As on January 1, 2018),* New Delhi, 2019, the graph on pp 27.

3. The percentage was placed before the *Lok Sabha* (The lower house of the parliament) by the Minister of State for Home Affairs, Shri Nityanand Rai on August 10, 2021.

4. *National Police Research Repository : Research Studies on Police and Prison Issues (1970 – 2016),* Published by Bureau of Police Research and Development, New Delhi, 2017, pp 27.

5. *National Police Research Repository, Golden Jubilee Edition : Research Studies on Police and Prison Issues (2016 – 2020)*, Published by Bureau of Police Research and Development, New Delhi, 2021, pp 8.

6. Lt Col M D Sharma, *Para Military Forces of India*, Kalpaz publications, Delhi, 2008, pp 90.

7. Anirudh Deshpande (Ed), *Glorious Fifty years of Border Security Force*, Shipra Publication, Delhi, India, 2015, pp11.

8. See Note 6, pp 31.

9. Kalpana, PhD (Psychology), *Working/Role of Women in CISF,* IOSR Journal of Humanities and Social Sciences, Vol 24, Issue 4, Serial 9, (April 2019) 01-04, pp 3

10. Ibid, pp 2.

11. See Note 6, pp 162.

12. For details see https://zeenews.india.com/india/crpf-s-elite-anti-terrorist-unit-valley-qat-to-have-women-commandos-soon-2346460.html (Accessed on December, 2021)

13. The Indian Express, *Women in ITBP : Striking Down Another Barrier?*, October 8, 2015.

14. The Times of India, *U'Khand gets all-women ATS commando squad,* February 25, 2021. pp 2nd half-fold.

CHAPTER - 7

"THE BROKEN GLASS CEILING": WOMEN IN THE ARMED FORCES, THE GLOBAL SCENE

"There is no force equal to a woman determined to rise."

W E B Du Bois
*(An American and Ghanaian sociologist,
civil rights activist, and a writer)*

The Overview

War is a sensational, violent, and the most deliberated socio-political activity of human beings. All through recorded history it has been and continues to be, the last resort to settle disputes. It has been, as the saying goes, *Ultima Ratio Regum*, [1] meaning 'the last argument of kings.' Be that as it may, in the contextual framework of this book, the point to be noted is that, for thousands of years, it had remained a men's preserve – society's deeply ingrained *idee fixe* that all aspects of war-waging commanded male attributes. Female abilities had been undermined. The opening chapter has already narrated the evolution of this gender role – the coming into being of the glass ceiling that had barred women from the profession of arms.

The change in the attitude, and behaviour of the societies the world over, took its own time. Earlier chapters have already illustrated how, starting mid-19th century, the discriminating barriers slowly lost their rigidity and how, by the end of the Second World War, the presence of women in uniform had gained wider acceptability.

By then they were no more there as 'adjunct' to the fighting men, nor were they there to be 'tolerated' in times of crisis. They were there to stay. In the second half of the 20th century, they had made further forays into the armed forces. As of now, there are close to fifty countries across the globe that have women in their armed forces – with non-combat responsibilities in most of them while some have also integrated them into the combat roles. The following text brings out some of those minutiae. While doing so only four countries are being addressed – two of them are of course from India's immediate neighbourhood, China and Pakistan, and the other two being USA and Israel who have led the pack with women in their armed forces in large numbers. There is also a short 'fact file' presenting some interesting details about a few other countries.

USA

United States (US) military has always been more progressive than most others, By the end of the Second World War, women in uniform had become a force to reckon with and their presence in the armed forces had generally been accepted as an enabling necessity. Not surprisingly, some of those who had been demobilized after WW-II were recalled for duty during the Korean War (1952-53). Later, as many as 11,000 of them served during the Vietnam War. Some of them also had the privilege of commanding sub-units there and one of them rose to become the first one-star general in the US Army. [2] By 1973 US Navy had six women pilots. A year later the Army had inducted its first female helicopter pilot and by 1977 the Air Force also had women flying its planes.

During the Gulf War (1990-91) women broke through some more barriers and their role and numbers increased at a brisker pace thereafter. Removal of some of the restraining clauses in 1993 opened many more avenues for women in the US Air Force. The removal of the 'Risk Rule' a year later allowed women to serve in almost all positions except those in direct combat. With that, women had an even more telling presence in the war zone – in Iraq in 2005, Leigh Ann Aster became the first one to be awarded a Silver Star for her bravery. By 2008 USA had its first woman four-star general – General Ann E Dunwoody.

Once the decision to remove the restrictions of 'combat exclusion' for women was taken in 2013 – it actually took effect only in 2015 – women could also be frontline soldiers. With all stops thus removed, some of them were soon attending Army's Ranger School and some others were making their way into Navy's SEAL (Sea Air and Land) Teams. In 2016 West Point had its first female Commandant of the Cadets and by 2019 there was a lady general commanding a National Guard Division. To crown it all, in December 2020, Capt Amy Bauernschmidt of the US Navy, an experienced pilot, took over the command of the nuclear-powered aircraft carrier USS Abraham Lincoln – one of the most powerful symbols of US military might. Need one say more about their spectacular progress and achievements?

As of now, there are about 17 percent women soldiers, sailors, and airmen in the US armed forces.

Israel

In the conservative societies of most of the Middle East countries, women lead the life of subservient homemakers, and quite often do so behind the veils. "In Israel, however, the prevailing attitudes towards a women's role in society are infinitely more 'liberal' and modern; in essence, they are more Occidental or European than Oriental. Nowhere it is better symbolized than by the role of women in the Israel Defense Forces." [3] (IDF)

David Bern Gurion, who in May 1948 had proclaimed the coming into being of the state of Israel, was of the firm opinion that women must enjoy equal rights and should also contribute as much to the state as men. Accordingly, a law was passed that mandated military service for all women above the age of 18. Israel thus became the first country in the world to exercise the option of mobilizing women – besides the men of course – even in peacetime. Further, in accordance with its policy, IDF created a Women's Corps (Hebrew acronym CHEN). The policy, besides empowering women with equal rights, was also of value in three other ways. Those being, one, it was a great unifying factor for the country, two, it helped in projecting IDF as 'People's Army' and three, it freed men for frontline duties – as the slogan goes "Another soldier in the Women's Corps is another soldier to the front."

Quite contrary to the common belief conscription is not all-inclusive and has many exceptions. Eligible aspirants are put through a rigorous selection process which, besides the stipulated educational standards, also includes intelligence, psychological, and fitness tests. Legal requirements apart, serving in the forces is a matter of pride for the young girls, and those who make the grade are treated as a 'set apart' by the society. To start with women soldiers were denied combat roles. In 1995 Israel's top court ruled that "Women could be drafted to combat roles as infantry combat soldiers, naval officers, combat soldiers in the Anti-Aircraft Defense Array, and more". [4] 'Equality Amendment to the Military Service Law', drafted by Israel's women lawmakers in 2000, states that "The right of women to serve in any role in the IDF is equal to the right of men." By 2006 IDF had formed an all-women reconnaissance company and the same year women in uniform were very much in action in combat roles in the Second Lebanon War. Even so, the said Law came up for examination again in 2014 and the oppositions apart, Major Oshrat Bachar became the first to be given the command of a combat unit. In 2018 a female pilot went on to become the commander of a flight squadron. As of now, about 85 percent of positions in the IDF are open to women.

It is noteworthy that, well over five hundred Israeli women soldiers have laid down their lives for the country so far.

China

People's Liberation Army (PLA) signifies the entire armed forces of the People's Republic of China and is the armed wing of the ruling Chinese Communist Party (CCP). Though Chairman Mao had once stated that "women hold up half the sky", implying women as a resource should be employed in various fields for nation-building, they had remained largely underrepresented in the Chinese armed forces. Not anymore. "Today the PLA is a nuclear-capable army that includes a potent missile force, with increasingly sophisticated weaponry, and which has become more 'Western' in its outlook." [5] In the recent past, one of the major impulses of PLA's transformation has been the last bit of the quote, 'western in its outlook', which has greatly added to women's numbers in various capacities and trades in all its five service branches. [6]

Women have gone past the stage of playing the traditional support role as medics, nurses, and communication operators. Young women with rising aspirations find opportunities in PLA as one of the preferred and prestigious options. Now they are there as tank crews, anti-aircraft missile firers, and after 2009 also as fighter pilots. There were reports about the raising of a specially trained all-women brigade. However, details about its possible deployment and employment have remained unclear. Be that as it may, by 2018 women were also forming part of the Special Force Teams and PLA's ground forces inducted the first batch of female helicopter pilots in 2021. Incidentally, a select band of women also form the Honour Guard of PLA and play a ceremonial role during military parades and events.

The ambitious reforms agenda for the PLA set in motion by Chairman Xi in early 2016 gives no clear indication of women's role in the new dispensation. Nevertheless, "China today is a society on the move" [7] and so are the Chinese women. With their presence in the Chinese armed forces, dragon's teeth may acquire some added sparkle without losing the cutting edge.

Pakistan

As early as in the 1940s Muhammad Ali Jinnah, the founder of Pakistan, had said "Be prepared to train women in combat; Islam does not want women to be shut up and never see fresh air." Maybe he was ahead of his time because the formal entry of women in the Pakistan armed forces commenced only after the turn of the 20th century; that too only as officers. Women are still not enrolled in rank and file in either of the three services. Admittedly, women have been serving in the medical corps even earlier. Shahida Malik for example, who was commissioned in 1970, and was decorated twice for her exemplary services, went on to become a major general in 2002 – first lady officer to be promoted as a general officer not only in the Pakistan army but also in all the other Muslim countries.

Pakistan Air Force (PAF) was first off the block to induct women when it started training a batch of women fighter pilots in 2003. On completion of their training, they were commissioned in the PAF in 2006. Close on its heels, the first lot of women cadets passed out from the Pakistan Military Academy in 2007. In the army, women officers are not commissioned in the three combat arms – infantry, armoured corps, and artillery. Similarly, the intake of women officers in the Pakistan Navy is also only in the technical, logistic, and administrative branches.

Over the years these women officers have gone from strength to strength. A select few of them were trained as paratroopers in 2013. Pakistani contingents for the UN peacekeeping mission usually have as many as 15 percent women in them. Pakistan Army's female 'Engagement Team' in Congo earned UN medals for their commendable efforts. And, in July 2020, Lieutenant General Nigar Johar, a three-star general, became the first lady officer to be appointed as the Surgeon General of the Pakistan Army. Remarkable indeed.

A 'Fact File'

Details below are not all-inclusive and are intended only to give a better idea of the existing global scene: -

- ➢ In Germany, women were allowed in combat roles in 2001. Now they serve as fighter pilots, paratroopers, and even onboard submarines.
- ➢ The UK permitted women in combat positions in the tank units and in the air force in 2016 and two years later all positions were thrown open to them.
- ➢ French women make up twenty percent of the armed forces with about two percent of them in combat units.

- As early as 1995 Norway became the first North Atlantic Treaty Organization (NATO) country to open doors for women to serve in any capacity – of course, subject to the selection criteria.

- The United Arab Emirates became the first in the Gulf Region to establish a Women's Military College in 1991 and its first fighter pilot, Maj Mariam Mansouri, made headlines when she flew a combat mission against the Islamic State of Iraq and Syria (ISIS). [8]

- North Korea resorts to selective conscription of women for a minimum of six years of service.

- Women won the battle of sexes when, in February 2021, conservative Saudi Arabia allowed the recruitment of women in the forces. [9]

- In October 2021 Kuwait opened doors for women to join armed forces in combat roles both as officers and in ranks. [10]

As an update to this Fact File, it is mentioned that, in the ongoing Russia-Ukraine War (March 2022 onwards), Ukrainian women from the threatened population centres have stepped forward to learn handling of AK-47 to be part of the civil defence. The media is also abuzz with the exploits of a Ukrainian female sharpshooter who is only known by her call-sign "Charcoal." Her actual identity and the details of her heroic deeds have not been made public so far. Also, Ukraine's Kristina Dmitrenko, who won a gold medal in the 2016 Olympics in Biathlon – an event that combines skiing cum shooting – intends to join the Ukrainian forces declaring, "I shoot well so the invaders will not have a chance". [11]

Conclusion

The following lines, written by a perceptive unknown author, aptly sum up what sets these women soldiers apart: -

"While you carry a purse, she carries a 65 lb rucksack.

While you shop with your girlfriends,

she cleans her rifle with her battle buddies.

When you wear heels, she wears her combat boots.

Instead of the make-up that you wear on your face to make yourself look pretty,

she paints her face for camouflage.

While you kiss your husband goodbye for the day,

she kisses her goodbye for the year."

All these daring women had to overcome centuries of unfair restrains and obstacles to reach where they have today. Even now, while in service, they face many situational problems – sexual harassment being one of the most worrying ones. [12] Nevertheless, with their determined and assertive ways they are already setting enviable standards in combat and command assignments not only in the developed nations but also in the developing ones and India has been no exception. Over the last three decades, Indian women have also made steady but forceful entry into the Indian armed forces – the central theme of the next chapter.

Endnotes

1. Inscription on the cannons of Louis XIV of France, 1643-1715.

2. For details see *Danielle DeSimone's write up in United Service Organization, USA, March 2021.*

3. Tom Bowden, *Army in the Service of the State*, University Publishing Projects, Tel Aviv, Israel, 1976, pp 94.

4. https://www.idf.il/en/minisites/idf-activity/the-history-of-women-in-the-idf/ (Accessed on January 8, 2022).

5. Benjamin Lai, *The Dragon's Teeth*, Casemate, Publishers, Havertown, PA, USA, pp 11.

6. The five major branches in the PLA are, the Army, Navy, Air Force, Rocket Force and the Strategic Support Force.

7. Kerry Brown, *Contemporary China*, Palgrave Macmillan, 2013, pp 129.

8. For more details on the first five countries mentioned above, see https://sg.news.yahoo.com/nine-countries-that-allow-women-in-combat-positions-081844202.html (Accessed on January 12, 2022).

9. The Times of India (Delhi edition), *Saudi women can now join armed forces,* February 22, 2021, pp 15.

10. The Times of India, (Delhi edition), *Kuwait Allows Women to Join Military in Combat Roles*, October 13, 2021, pp 24.

11. https://www.ndtv.com/world-news/russia-ukraine-war-olympic-star-shooter-joins-ukraine-forces-warns-russian-troops-they-wont-have-a-chance-2978011. (Accessed on May 16, 2022)

12. See Maj Gen Mrinal Suman, AVSM, VSM, Phd, *Women in the Indian Armed Forces,* Indian Defence Review, Jul-Sep 2006, Vol 21, box stories on pp 92, 93, and 94.

CHAPTER - 8

"THE SHATTERED GLASS CEILING": WOMEN IN THE ARMED FORCES, THE INDIAN SCENE

"The domestic career is no more natural to all women than the military career is natural to all men.".

– *George Bernard Shaw*

Trooping into the Male Stronghold

The notion that the profession of arms is a man's calling, is deeply ingrained in the Indian psyche for two main reasons. First, the patriarchal Indian society remains convinced that nature had created women to nurture life and that the gender roles had been determined biologically. Second, the *Varna* system – the social order of ancient India – had entrusted *Kshatriya men* (emphasis on *men* added) to bear arms to protect society. That a *Kshatriya* is honour bound to perform his duty was also articulated by Lord Krishna when, at the beginning of the battle in *Mahabharat*, he reminded indecisive Arjun by saying "Considering your specific duty as *Kshatriya* you should know that there is no better engagement for you than fighting on religious principles and so there is no need for hesitation." [1] Thus, enjoined by the scriptures, men of this warrior class continued to bear arms and excel in the martial arts for centuries. The system remained in place till the recent past. It was set to change.

Cut to the present times. Just before Independence, in March 1947, Lord Wavell, the outgoing Viceroy of India, had said "I believe that the stability of the Indian Army may perhaps be the deciding factor in the future of India." [2] So indeed has been the case. Ever since Independence, Indian armed forces have unflinchingly risen to the occasion to ward off threats from without and to ensure stability within. They are admired by the citizenry for their professional excellence, sacrifices and for their apolitical nature. A career in the Indian armed forces has an élan of its own and it appeals to the Indian youth – men and women alike.

That said, according to the Army and the Air Force Acts of 1950, and that of the Indian Navy of 1957, women were not eligible for the armed forces – neither as commissioned officers nor as enlisted men – and only a government waiver could allow them to serve in the specified branches/departments. Accordingly, permission for the permanent commission (PC) to the lady doctors in all three Services was granted in 1958. Everything else continued to remain off-limits for them. The issue of enlisting them in other positions and capacities came up for serious consideration only when the matters of women's empowerment and gender equality picked up steam in India in the second half of the last century. Consequently, the ground breaking decision to allow women in the armed forces was taken in July 1992. To start with, women officers were to be granted short service commissions (SSC) [3] and they could serve only in the select few logistic and administrative branches of the army, navy and air force. This cautious start by the armed forces opened the floodgates for the enterprising young Indian women who had been waiting in the wings for the clue to make their entry. Their initial trickle soon turned into a spate and they have not looked back ever since. The following text delves deeper into their 'quick march' into this male stronghold.

Officers Training Academy (OTA) at Chennai has been imparting pre-commission training to male SSC officers for long, and women cadets were also to be trained there. [4] Accordingly, the first batch of 25 women cadets reported at the OTA in September 1992. As against the usual training period of 44 weeks, it was curtailed to 24 weeks for them and the existing physical standards and outdoor exercises were suitably modified. The navy and the air force also made similar adjustments in their training syllabi and schedules. For example, the navy organized seamanship training of naval cadets on INS Vikrant – it was then berthed in the dockyard – without quartering women cadets on board since it was not possible administratively. However, all such teething troubles were promptly addressed and overcome by all the three Services in their usual efficient ways. Further, besides the twice-yearly entrance examination conducted by the Union Public Service Commission, other avenues were also thrown open for women's entry – through National Cadet Corps, as technical graduates and as law qualified candidates. In this regard, two points merit a mention. First, women aspirants were given no special status or concessions and they had to compete with their male counterparts. Thus, the entire selection process was strictly merit-based. Second, their intake remained as SSC officers only.

Nevertheless, neither the tough competition nor the restricted tenure of duty dampened the spirit of the women officers who soon notched up many firsts. Capt Alka Khurana became the first woman officer to participate both in the Army Day and the Republic Day parades in 1994. Capt Ruchi Sharma, commissioned in 1996, was the first one who opted to be a paratrooper and successfully made her para-jump in 1997. Women officers had taken wings in the IAF too. Flight Lieutenant Gunjan Saxena was among the first few helicopter pilots to fly operational sorties in the combat zone during the Kargil War of 1999. [5] Squadron Leader Deepika Misra became the first woman pilot to join 'Sarang' – IAF's helicopter display team that demands extreme flying precision. There were many other first-timers too. For example, in 2010, Divya Ajith outdid all her batchmates in OTA – 244 gentlemen and women cadets – to be adjudged the best all-round cadet and to be awarded the coveted Sword of Honour. However, the text is not being cluttered further with their manifold achievements.

Some Recent Developments

Having come into their own, and made their mark in various fields, the denial of PC continued to rankle women officers – both the serving ones and the would-be. Even after the army started granting

PC to female officers in 2008 in its Legal and the Education Corps, women continued to question the rationale for not being accepted in other arms and services, including the ones with combat roles. The armed forces had strong reservations on the issue of combat roles for women on many counts – more about it a little later. Occasional sly remarks such as "An officer who cannot run with us, cannot train with us and cannot exercise with us can barely be expected to lead us" [6] conveyed an unmistakable sense of men's unease. Even so, set of reservations notwithstanding, IAF took the bold step in 2015 to accept women as fighter pilots. By 2019 three bright and determined women trainees had qualified as fighter pilots and were cleared to fly operational missions. They had truly lived up to the IAF's motto *"Nabhah Sparsham Diptam"*, meaning "Touch the Sky with Glory". Alongside the IAF, the navy too had its first woman pilot flying maritime surveillance missions.

A group of female SSC officers, who had been denied PC after 14 years of active service, had filed a case against the decision in the Supreme Court (SC). The court did not find merit in the arguments placed before it by the government and, in February 2020, ruled in favour of the petitioners observing that the denial of PC and command assignments to women officers was discriminatory. Unfolding events then led to the army allowing PC to women officers in eight more corps but none in the combat arms. The navy was also against the idea of having women on board warships. The issue of combat role remained a bone of contention and the women were unafraid to take a leap of faith.

Apropos the desired changes, the year 2021 was certainly 'the year of the reckoning' since that year, the SC intervened more than once to pass landmark judgements in favour of women. In March 2021, female officers in the army won their case when the SC ruled that the standards of fitness laid down for them were 'arbitrary' and 'irrational'. While upholding the point of 'equality' for female officers, the honourable Court had wisely differentiated between women being 'equal' but not 'identical' to men. In another interim order passed in August 2021, the Court allowed women to appear for the National Defence Academy (NDA) entrance examination observing that the "exclusion of females will be a hurdle in their career." [7] The Court then followed it up by refusing to accept the Center's proposal to postpone it to the next year. "We do not want to deny them (women aspirants) once we have given them hope," the Bench said. [8] The government had to agree to implement the Court's directions. Women kept up their good fight and only a month later the Centre had to file an affidavit in the SC stating that the Rashtriya Indian Military College (RIMC) and all other military schools will also be thrown open for the girls.

Two other events of the year 2021 also merit a mention. First, in July of that year army decided to induct women helicopter pilots into its Army Aviation Corps. This shift in the army's policy was also mentioned by the Chief of the Army Staff while addressing the India Today Conclave in October 2021 in New Delhi. Second, that year army also welcomed its first draft of 83 women soldiers in the Corps of Military Police. The army's long-term plan aims to have a total of 1700 of them in a phased manner over the years

The government and the armed forces came under pressure once again when, in January 2022, on the basis of the plea filed before it, the SC sought the government's response why only 19 female cadets had been admitted to each of the first two NDA courses. Gauging the Court's intent, in the next hearing on March 8, 2022 – it was International Women's Day – the government submitted that "there has been a change of mindset" and that the forces were ready to induct more women officers. [9] Independent of the foregoing case of NDA, in March 2022, it was reported that five girls would be joining RIMC – the most prestigious feeder institute for NDA – in the next academic session. [10] Similarly, all the Sainik Schools were also gearing up to accept the girl students. What's more, on January 8, 2022, while chairing a webinar on Sainik Schools, Defence Minister Shri Rajnath Singh announced "100 new Sainik Schools to provide more opportunities for girls to join armed forces." [11]

According to the government "There are 9,118 women currently serving the army, navy, and the air force, with the services giving them more opportunities to boost career progression - - - - the government has taken a raft of measures to empower women, including allowing them to fly fighter planes, naval aircraft and giving them a permanent commission in different branches - - - - the army accounts for 6,807 women officers, the air force 1,607 and the navy 704 women officers." [12] The figures are for early 2021 and may have recorded an upward change. According to the government's submission before the SC, as of March 2022, women accounted for 13.6 per cent of the Indian armed forces officer's cadre. Just for the sake of comparison, it is mentioned that three other countries have higher percentages of women officers in their defence forces with the USA in the lead at 17 per cent. [13]

In Sum

As of now, Indian women are only a small fraction of one of the largest armed forces in the world. The playing field has been uneven for them. They have faced more dissensions than acceptances. There is still a long way to go for them and there are rough patches ahead. Yet, just as the kite rises high only against the wind, so have they soared high against the restraining odds. Over the years they have excelled and prevailed in all their endeavours. They are now there to stay and are set to enlarge their telling presence at a pace faster than hitherto. All along they were driven by their passion not just to get into the profession of arms *per se,* but to change the game itself. All three Services would do well to reorient and restructure the forces keeping in mind the women cadres, and the citizenry would do well to applaud these uniformed women who have shattered the glass ceiling. They deserve as much if not more respect than men

It transpires that the ongoing influx of women in the militaries across the globe, signifying the 'regendering' of the armed forces in general, and the female accession to the combat roles in particular, has raised a set of some weighty questions. Is the move in the right direction? Have the changes been one too many and too fast? Have the aspects of the unit's cohesion and the combat potential of the force been fully visualized? The next chapter discusses these issues *sans* prejudices.

Endnotes

1. A C Bhaktivedanta Swami Prabhupada, *Bhagvada Geeta As It Is*, Bhaktivedanta Book Trust, Mumbai 1998, pp 115.

2. Rajesh Kadian, *India and its Army*, Vision Books Pvt Ltd, New Delhi, 1990, Foreword.

3. A contractual period of five years which is extendable to a maximum of fourteen years.

4. OTA also trains women cadets from other friendly foreign countries, including Afghanistan.

5. A biopic on her, named *Gunjan Saxena : The Kargil Girl*, was released in August 2020. It drew flak from the IAF for incorrect and damaging picturization.

6. Maj Gen Mrinal Suman, AVSM, VSM, Phd, *Women in the Indian Armed Forces*, Indian Defence Review, Jul-Sep 2006, Vol 21, pp 94.

7. The Times of India (Delhi edition), *In Equality Push, SC Allows Women to take NDA Exam*, August 19, 2021, pp 1 and 8.

8. The Times of India (Delhi edition), *Admit Women to NDA From This Yr Itself*, September 23, 2021, pp 1 and 15.

9. The Times of India (Delhi edition), *Mindset changed, forces can induct more women : Govt*, March 9, 2022, opposite pp 1.

10. The Times of India, (Delhi edition) *In a 1st, 100-yr-old RIMC to open its doors for girls*, March 14, 2022, pp 11.

11. India Strategic, Vol 17, Issue 1, January 2022, New Delhi, India.

12. For details see https://wsimag.com/economy-and-politics/66942-women-in-indian-armed-forces-she-is-unique (Accessed on February 4, 2022).

13. The Times of India, (Delhi edition), *13.6% defense officers women, govt tells SC*, March 9, 2022, pp 1.

CHAPTER – 9

WOMEN IN COMBAT ROLE: A HOLISTIC RÉSUMÉ OF RESERVATIONS AND CONCERNS

First, they ignore you,
Then they laugh at you,
Then they fight you,
Then you win.

– Mahatma Gandhi

The Backdrop

From the Armenian War of 1853-56 to the post-WW-II period, women had taken more than a century to incrementally prove their abilities and relevance to establish a firm footing amongst those who bear arms. Their entry was neither through the by-lane or the backyard but from the front door. Maybe no red carpets were rolled out for them, but they had certainly stepped over the 'welcome' doormat to enter. The pace of their growing numbers and the process of their integration into the civil police, CAPFs, and the armed forces have thrown up several professional and administrative challenges. While addressing those, the role and the desirability of women and their rising aspirations is one of the most hotly debated topics within these organizations and amongst social scientists and scholars. The core question of women in the combat roles in the three services – the army, navy, and the air force – has attracted their attention the most. If there are enough women's commissions, non-government organizations (NGO), celebrated women activists, and even male feminists quoting constitutional rights and championing women's cause in favour of the move, there are equally strong lobbies and voices opposing the government policies and questioning the court rulings with genuine concerns. Their weighty arguments cannot be wished away. Interestingly, there are men and women on both sides of the divide.

Be that as it may, this chapter aims to discuss various facets of the reservations as a critique *sans* blinder. The ensuing discussion is armed forces centric and it is hoped that such misgivings that the civil police and the para-military forces may have on the subject will also get suitably addressed. To better understand the discussion of the core issue – concerns related to the combat role for women in the armed forces – a word about the overarching importance of the armed forces in the national security narrative is necessary.

Defence forces signify the sword arm of the state and, as the ultimate guarantors of national security, their faltering or failure in war may well be a poser for the very existence or the extermination of the state. Sun Tzu, the scholarly Chinese general, in his masterly work *The Art of War*, had rightly stated that "Warfare is the greatest affair of the state - - - - The province of life and death; the road to survival or ruin." In that context, it must also be appreciated that war-waging is a ruthless activity and a battlefield is an unforgiving place. An enemy will show no mercy only because some of its adversaries are women. Exposé in Appendix F drives home the point that there are no gender-neutral battlefields. Not surprisingly, India's former Chief of Naval Staff, Admiral Arun Prakash, has no doubts that "The army's job is to provide national security and not gender equality" and Heather Mac Donald, an American scholar, is convinced that "Women don't belong in combat units" and that "It is a misguided social experiment."[1] The discussion that follows is developed against this backdrop.

Contours of Reservations and Concerns

The first one relates to the mental barrier. The image of a soldier that an average citizen carries is that of a well-built tough-looking man, often with handlebar mustaches and intimidating body language. Similarly, one conjures up a sailor as a bearded man with tattooed arms and a naval cap donned at a jaunty angle. An officer is usually pictured as a man with a bit of a gruff countenance, military accoutrements embellishing his uniform, and who barks orders that must be obeyed unquestioningly. How many women fit into this description? Do they appear in any one of these frames? Whereas they do come to mind as nurses, radio operators, and clerical staff, it is still difficult to readily visualize a woman in camouflaged fatigues with a blackened face carrying battle loads and an assault rifle in the crook of her arm. That too despite the fact that they have been in the armed forces, in increasingly great numbers and capacities, for more than a century since the Great War.

"It was not uncommon during the First World War for women who joined the military services to be regarded as peculiar at least, if not downright immoral." [2] It was certainly an unfair judgment-in-rem. Similarly, "In many reports, women's armed activism is directly linked to perceived sexual deviance." [3] Even during the Second World War, the enrolment of women for military service was strongly contested. "More visceral resisters posited that women would not be able to accept military discipline and that inducting women would 'masculine' them - - - -." [4] Though the contentions were a bit too far-fetched, the prospects of possible 'masculinity' – whether physical, attitudinal, or behavioural – were unwelcome to both the sexes. That apart, the contentions were indicative of society's unease – women performing military service was a disturbing idea to many. *Idée fixe* of those opposing women's entry may have also been influenced by the famous dialogue of that time "War is men's business, not ladies" from the movie *Gone With the Wind* –1939 classic that had bagged ten Academy Awards from thirteen nominations.

Thus, despite evidence to the contrary, the widely held belief, stated explicitly by the anthropologist Lionel Tiger, remains that "almost universally, war is an all-male enterprise." [5] By and large, people still connect aggression and violence with men and peace and tranquility with women and it is difficult to think of women in a combat role. There is also the point of male soldiers' aversion to being led and ordered by women officers in battle. The unease may be even more pronounced in the Indian context where the vast majority of male soldiery comes from the rural background – particularly so in the army – and is influenced by the strong undercurrents of patriarchal culture.

The second issue stems from the fact that men, compared to women, being hardier and more aggressive by nature, are more suited for the professional demands and hazards of soldiering. Because of sexual dimorphism – signifying the physical difference between males and females of the same species – men are typically bigger compared to women and are heavier in build with greater bone mass and more muscles. It makes them much stronger than women. According to the Centre for Military Readiness, an American NGO, "Female soldiers are, on average, shorter and smaller than men, with 45-50% less upper body *strength* and 25-30% less aerobic capacity, which is essential for *endurance*". (Emphasis added). [6] Studies also show that both male and female soldiers make similar gains during training, but the relative difference between their different take-off points remains unchanged. Physical differences apart, men and women also differ vastly in their outlook on life. The title of American writer John Gray's book, "*Men Are from Mars, Women Are from Venus*" says it all.

"Of all human activities war is by far the most nasty and the most dangerous. Physically, it is also the most demanding." [7] Since one cannot fight nature, women will always remain disadvantaged in trying to match men's strength and stamina – whether on the rifle range or the obstacle course. Lowering physical standards for women, or watering them down to make them gender-neutral, can only degrade the combat capabilities of a force. Acknowledging these biological realities, one of the concepts mooted is that of 'equivalency' which focuses on maximizing the contributing qualities of individuals. [8] The concept has been contested on the grounds that "women cannot be regarded as fully equal in a Corps that prioritizes physical strength." [9]

A school of thought maintains that, with the fast pace of technological advancements, the rigid requirements of physical standards could well be brought down by many notches. Soldiering to them is so much more brain than brawn. But then, the options and opportunities that technological sophistications offer must not be mistaken for the combat roles that the women are seeking. In war-waging, technology does not take away the requirement of physical fitness, mental robustness, and aggressive spirit of the frontline troops – the boots on the ground, the glint of the bayonet. Surely, while fighting around Kyiv in Ukraine (March-April 2022), elite Russian troops faltered despite their hi-tech backup for some such reasons, besides of course the Ukrainian resistance. That apart, the need for physical effort is also determined by the nature of the military's visualized operational commitments. In the Indian context for example, because of the hostile terrain along its far-flung and troubled borders – snow-bound mountains, high altitudes, extreme conditions on the Siachen Glacier, and the teeming jungles of some of its insurgency prone northeastern states – the importance of physical fitness of the man-power intensive Indian forces cannot be over-emphasized.

There is also the question of women's ability to withstand the protracted physical and mental stress – the blood and gore – of the contact warfare. During an interview with a news channel on women in a combat role, late Gen Bipin Joshi, the former Chief of Defence Staff, mentioned that "Women would feel uncomfortable at the front line." As is well-known, in adverse situations when the chips are down, the physically and mentally tough troops carry the day. It must also be remembered that, while both male and female PsOW may be ill-treated by the captor, women soldiers are likely to be abused with a vengeance.

The next set of concerns presents a mixed bag of interconnected issues of co-existence, integration, unit cohesion, and combat readiness.

The co-existence of women soldiers in combat units implies the presence of a handful of young and fit women living, working, and feeding together amongst a much larger number of men in their prime. When so billeted, women soldiers experience a lack of privacy and poor comfort level – more so in the cramped spaces onboard a ship or a submarine – and also feel stressed in the environment of male culture. Men expect 'sameness' from female soldiers and in its absence, there is a degree of resistance to their acceptance in the unit. Women rarely manage to break into the 'boys' circle' and often experience workplace aggression out of it. Further, quite contrary to the desirable individual sexual restrain, women attract unwanted male attention giving rise to sexual competition and even triggering sexual arousal. Military regulations, and the laid down code of conduct notwithstanding, nature cannot be ordered and the basic male instincts rule the roost. Since female soldiers possess what is being sought after, they – some by design and most others unwittingly – exercise a degree of hold over the competing males. The fallouts of such a slapdash setting – of link-ups, relationships, break-ups, or the cases of sexual harassment and/or assault – are bad for seamless gender integration.

In military parlance, the term 'unit cohesion' refers to the unqualified bonds of professional trust and shared commitment amongst the soldiers that collectively motivate them for mission accomplishment against all odds. It makes or breaks a unit. It goes without saying that the distractions of a sex-skewed environment referred to above can only have adverse effects on a unit's discipline and camaraderie. According to a noted scholar and defense analyst "Men and women really like each other and will distract each other enough to ruin unit cohesion and thereby military effectiveness." [10] Further, it is also true that the armed forces are expected to remain war-ready even when the remainder nation may be at peace. "The military's inherent self-image is that of a specialist in violence, ready to combat." [11] In that sense, issues of pregnancy, maternity leave, and motherhood are not compatible with military service either.

A digression is necessary here to mention that the para-military forces, armed constabularies, civil police, and even the firefighters voice similar concerns about women's proliferating numbers and roles in their respective organizations.

Returning to the point of digression, and before closing this discussion, one more viewpoint merits a mention. Martin Van Creveld, an Israeli military historian, and theorist has a thought-provoking take on the subject of women's influx into the militaries.

In his article titled *Women in the Military: Gain or Regression,* [12] he argues that the politico-military cost of full-scale wars has become increasingly prohibitive and therefore the "Militaries of the developed countries are in full retreat." [13] The term 'retreat' refers to the scaling down of their threat perceptions, downsizing of the forces, and the progressive cuts in their defence budgets. The arguments have been substantiated with facts and figures. However, in the contextual framework of this chapter, the noteworthy aspect of 'retreat' is the observation that the force reductions have been in inverse proportion to the number of women in it – while the total strength of the force came down, the number of women therein increased. He contends that, in absence of military threats, the "Regular armed forces of most developed states are ceasing to be warfighting machines" [14] and are preparing for missions other than the traditional ones. An increasing number of women from such countries "Are entering the military precisely *because* they hope they will not be obliged to fight" [15] and those countries are not particularly disturbed by the trend since, as the saying goes, "Anyone can hold the helm when the sea is calm." The author also maintains that, unlike women from the developed nations, those from the troubled third world countries, who know the vagaries of war, are staying away from such ventures.

Positive Aspects of Women In the Uniform

Women have always been there in the militaries in one form or the other – informally or formally. During the two World Wars, when their services were sought to tide over the manpower shortages, they had unhesitatingly donned the uniform to help the war efforts. In the more recent times, the armed forces are throwing open their doors to women for two main reasons – a rising sense of individuality and aspirations of women seeking equal opportunities including their 'right to fight', and the changing nature of war throwing open increasing opportunities for women combatants. Gender-specific problems apart, the following pluses of their attitudes and capabilities must not be overlooked: -

> ➢ Women who opt for combat roles do so with full knowledge of the professional hardships.

➢ Because of their high level of motivation, she-soldiers are most unlikely to 'belly ache' and shirk work.

➢ Women find few distractions at work and execute their tasks sincerely, safely, and accurately.

➢ Technological advancements, and the tenets of non-contact warfare, allow numerous positions for women combatants. For example, a person can effectively coordinate the fire of multiple and widely separated ground, sea, and air-based weapon systems from a well-appointed command post, or one can launch a cyber-attack on the enemy from the comfort of an operations room far removed from the battlefield. And such a person could well be a lady in uniform.

➢ Women soldiers have an important role to play in bridging the gap with the locals – women and children in particular – when engaged in the United Nations peace-keeping missions and/or while combating insurgency.

In short, as long as a person is qualified, gender should not matter. Besides, women combatants do possess quite a few qualities different and superior to those of men and their integration can only increase the talent pool of the forces.

In Sum

The 'regendering' of armed forces, with equal opportunities for both men and women, including those in combat arms, is a complex issue with wide ramifications. It is full of promises and pitfalls in equal measures. Though women's entrée into the combat arms has been incremental, in no country has their acceptance been without problems and, all along, their professionalism was mostly overlooked. Now that they are eyeing combat roles and are ready to dive deep in a submarine or fly high to rule the skies, the militaries are apprehensive of turning Nelson's eye to the fallouts hurting its combat potential – issues of physical capabilities, force integration, unit cohesion, and rigors of combat cannot be overlooked. No wonder, discussions, debates, and studies on the subject have remained dichotomous. Though the *raison d'être* of the armed forces is to remain ultimate guarantors of national security, and not to champion women's cause of equality, as an institution, it is high time it suitably modified its norms and practices to accommodate women for force enhancement. While the militaries are grappling with the problem, those who are forcefully championing the women's cause would do well to make haste slowly, and those vehemently opposed would do well to entertain the thought afresh with an open mind. Surely the truth – balancing and defining women's roles in the armed forces – lies somewhere in between.

As to India is concerned, "The constitution of India not only grants equality to women but also empowers the state to adopt measures of positive discrimination in favour of women." [16] Even so, faced with a set of serious and persisting external and internal threats, Indian political masters and the military brass will need to exercise extreme caution on this count.

With that, it is time to make some general observations and comments on women's emerging role and status in society.

Endnotes

1. Ms. Mac Donald is a fellow at the Manhattan Institute and has written extensively on the subject of females joining the armed forces in the USA.

2. Margaret Randolph Hingonnet, Jane Jenson, Sonya Michel, Margaret Collins Weitz (Ed), *Behind the Lines : Gender and the Two World Wars,* Yale University Press, New Haven and London, 1987, pp 121.

3. Nicole Detraz, *International Security and Gender,* Polity Press, Cambridge, UK, 2012, pp 112.

4. Rita James Simon (Ed), *Women in the Military,* Transaction Publishers, New Brunswick (USA) and London (UK), 1998, pp 7.

5. Lionel Tiger, *Men in Groups,* Thomas Nelson, London, UK, pp 80.

6. https://qforquestions.com/essay-on-inclusion-of-women-in-armed-forces/ (Accessed on April 02, 2022).

7. Stuart A Cohen (Ed), *Democratic Societies And Their Armed Forces : Israel In Comparative Context*, Frank Cass Publishers, London, UK, 2000, pp145.

8. For a detailed discussion of the concept, see Connie Brownson, *The Battle for Equivalency : Female US Marines Discuss Sexuality, Physical Fitness, and Military Leadership,* Armed Forces & Society 2014, Vol. 40(4) 765-788, Reprints and permission: sagepub.com/journalsPermissions.nav.

9. See Anthony C. King, *Women Warriors: Female Accession to Ground Combat, Armed Forces & Society,* 2015, Vol.41(2) 379-387, Reprints and permission: sagepub.com/journalsPermissions.nav.

10. https://warontherocks.com/2014/11/dont-exclude-women-from-combat-units-because-of-cohesion/ (Accessed on April 22, 2022).

11. See Note 7, pp 11.

12. It appears as Chapter 7 in Stuart A Cohen (Ed), *Democratic Societies And Their Armed Forces : Israel In Comparative Context,* Frank Cass Publishers, London, UK, 2000, pp135-149.

13. See Note 12, pp 135.

14. Ibid, pp 135.

15. Ibid, pp 142.

16. Dr. Om Raj Singh Vishnoi, *Women Police in India,* Aravali Printers and Publishers (P) Ltd, New Delhi 1999, pp 15

CHAPTER - 10

THE NEW EVE: AN AFTERWORD

"To call woman the weaker sex is a libel; it is man's injustice to woman."

– Mahatma Gandhi

The New Eve

Till as recent as only a century or so ago, young girls were generally groomed to be good home-makers. Their lives used to remain oriented to a multitude of household chores and childcare. "The notion that a woman's place was not in a career, and certainly not in politics, but in the home was expressed with fervour by such varied groups as moralists, exponents of advanced thoughts and tunesmiths". [1] If that was the Victorian idea in the western world, it was even more deeply ingrained in the oriental societies. Islamic fundamentalists of course had the strictest ideas on the subject with rigid dress regulations, a restraining code of conduct, and laws that allowed few liberties to women if any. Be that as it may, most women used to happily adjust to the prevailing social norms, and few who found it a bit stifling and grumbled were generally frowned upon. Those who stepped out to work did so out of necessity and usually found only gender-oriented employment as school teachers, receptionists, stenographers, nurses, and domestic help.

As mentioned earlier, women's exposures and experiences of the two world wars were their 'eureka moments' of self-realization. As a result, by the mid-twentieth century, they had stood up against the disparaging male attitudes and had challenged the traditional gender roles during the cultural revolution of the 1960s. A couple of decades later, the Women's Rights Movement of the 1980s, ushered in a degree of equality in workplaces that were traditionally male-dominated. Socially and economically the world has changed a lot since then. Societies have also become more liberal. Women have entered the twenty-first century backed by the fast pace of industrialization and globalization. There is also the 'push' of information technology. "The world has changed for women. Now it is time for women to start changing the world." [2]

While the changes in women's lifestyles and roles are more visible in developed countries, the reach of social media is causing ripples even in developing ones. Societies are astir everywhere with women's rising aspirations. There is a new eve on the starting block; rearing to go with big dreams and great expectations. However, "Gender inequalities continue to exist throughout the world through deceptively subtle forms of inequality." [3] Half the human race continues to be discriminated against, and/or neglected, on all counts of social justice – health, education, employment, wages, representation in public life, legal status, and so on. It is a moot question whether women have indeed stepped out of the 'Golden Cage' to enter the 'Golden Age' or is it a simple case of 'More things change, more they remain the same'? Relying on a few general observations, and with no claims to comprehensiveness, this chapter attempts a quick reality check.

Women on the Upswing: A General World Watch

Women are refusing to let others write their stories and are breaking into traditional male strongholds. Just as they have made their mark in the profession of arms, so are they making their presence felt in other fields too.

Take for instance politics. For the most part, women had little or no representation in politics or public life. In fact, they did not even enjoy voting rights – at the turn of the nineteenth century, there was only one country, New Zealand, where women had voting rights like men. [4] The second half of the twentieth century saw their presence in the local politics, a few on the national stage, and of course three very illustrious PMs – Golda Mier in Israel, Margaret Thatcher in the UK, and Indira Gandhi in India. As of now, that is in the year 2022, nine countries have women heads of state and fourteen of them have lady PMs. [5] Finland's cabinet is women predominant. In September 2021, the people of Iceland elected female-majority parliament. [6] Consequent to the elections in March 2022, 14 out of 22 ministers in the Dutch government are women. In May 2022, President Emanuel Macron of France appointed Elisabeth Borne as the PM of the French Republic, and the new Australian government, formed in June 2022, has 13 women ministers. In India, women have held the office of the President, the PM, Chief Ministers of various states, and have often been union ministers too. The current Indian parliament has 78 women parliamentarians (just about 15%) and 11 female ministers – the highest ever since the Independence.

Thus, women are in a comparatively happier space now. However, what is noteworthy is that there are many rough patches in their path to politics. Even now, they make up less than 25 % of lawmakers worldwide. Despite their tact and poise in the combative political environment, their capabilities are doubted and they are usually assigned less important portfolios. Being fewer in numbers their voices go unheard and their contribution unnoticed. At times they themselves go unnoticed as happened to Ursula Von Der Leyen, the first woman to head the European Commission, during her official visit to Turkey in April 2021. For a formal meeting with President Erdogan of Turkey, a chair was placed for her male colleague of equal status but not for her. Commenting on the oversight she asked, "How far we still have to go before women are treated as equals." [7]

All these years it was usual to associate business with business*men*, not business*women*. There is a noticeable shift in that perception with women coming into their own in the corporate sector too. They are now aiming for higher positions. Presently 41 companies from the Fortune 500 list have women Chief Executive Officers (CEO) leading such reputed companies as General Motors, Lockheed Martin the aerospace company, U Tube the video-sharing platform, and CVS Health – the highest-ranking business ever run by a woman. 15 Indian women are CEOs or Managing Directors of leading global companies like Chanel, Biocon, and IBM India.

A mention must also be made of Indira Nooyi, the former CEO of PepsiCo.

There are other diverse fields where women are making their presence felt. Here are some recent achievers and newsmakers: -

- Sian Hayley "Leo" Proctor successfully piloted the first all-civilian mission aboard Space X as a commercial astronaut in September 2021.
- In April 2022 Ketanji Brown Jackson went on to become the first black woman judge in the US Supreme Court.
- Nikhat Zareen, an Indian amateur boxer from a conservative Muslim family, punched her way to become world boxing champion in her weight category in May 2022. Just for the records, she had also won a gold medal in the junior world boxing championship in 2011.
- May 2022 also saw Saudi Arabian Airlines successfully operate its first domestic flight with an 'all-women crew'.
- About the same time in India, the top three ranks in the Civil Services Examination – arguably the toughest and most competitive – were secured by women candidates.
- In Iran women mechanics have broken through Tehran's male-dominated auto industry.
- Yuka Maedokaro, a celebrated Japanese bartender, is making waves with her off-the-beat passion to make the world's best absinthe – one of the strongest alcohols derived from several plants and herbs, and seasoned with flowers, and leaves of a moderately poisonous shrub, Artemisia Absinthium.

Like Yuka Maedokaro, quite a few women entrepreneurs are also venturing into fields less explored to live their dreams – as wine testers and bartenders, chefs and hoteliers, fitness experts, organic farmers, investment bankers, producers of shapewear and exotic cosmetics, and, hold your breath, also into the business of breast milk.

Women executives and entrepreneurs show some distinct traits. They are good team builders and evolve with time. They are born multi-taskers, and, therefore good coordinators and consolidators. Their decisions usually have a streak of originality with 'head for business and heart for the community'. Similarly, they tend to give equal emphasis not only on 'how much' they sell but also on 'what' they sell. They also insist on fair trade practices and are better borrowers. Even so, as in politics, women do face some problems and resistance in the corporate sector too. For example, female employees often get less paid compared to their male counterparts – Google has settled a lawsuit by agreeing to pay $ 118 million to its more than 15 thousand women employees who were paid less than men for the same job. [8] Being considerably smaller in number in the male-dominated business circles, women do not get opportunities to 'network' and tend to lose out in absence of enough 'contacts'. Though aptitude for business, grasp of finance, and/or marketing skills are not gender-specific, the business world is apt to take women with a pinch of salt as if they do not belong there. Nevertheless, as far as women are concerned, they mean business – pun not intended – and are carrying on regardless.

Whatever the field, by far the biggest challenge women professionals face is that of 'work-life balance'. The new eve expects, gender equality at home. Though working couples have started dividing the time-honoured family roles of parenting and housekeeping between the two partners, working women are weighed down by what society unfairly expects of them – to do a second shift at home after the day's hard work. Based on her own experiences, Ann Marie Slaughter, a reputed American international lawyer, in her article titled "No, Women Can't Have It All" has this to say "As evident then, 'having it all' is a phrase used exclusively in the context of women who juggle a professional career (typically high paying and respectable one) with a family, without having to sacrifice one for another. It is often seen as an ideal that women aspire to and only a select few can achieve - - - -." [9] It is high time society got rid of its self-comforting construct that a family is best off when the husband provides and the wife takes care of the home and the child/children. Even President Xi Jinping of China is of the opinion that "Women should take care of the elderly, educate children, and uphold family virtues of the Chinese nation." [10] Such statements do no justice to women or their aspirations.

No wonder, women have started raising their voices against inequality and stereotypes, and are not prepared to give a *carte blanche* to the menfolk in any field. They have a battle on hand.

A Brief on the Women's Woes

It is time to take a quick look at the regressive laws, attitudes, and traditions that continue to hold women down. Here again, only some of the ills are being reflected upon, that too briefly, to give an idea of women's woes in societies that, weighed down by the trappings of their own authority, refuse to budge. Most of the examples in the succeeding paragraphs are Indo-centric.

To start with the institution of marriage. It is a culturally and legally recognized union. The practice and the rituals vary in different cultures and regions. Save for the developed democracies where women enjoy equal rights, they have little or no say in arranged marriages and certainly none in child marriages or forced marriages. Similarly, women have no say in societies and religions that allow polygamy – it is allowed in Islam for example. With no options and choices, some get hitched into constricting or oppressive unions, face harassment on account of *Dowry* (Bridewealth), and miss out on the affection, intimacy, and the joys of married life. Some who dare to marry outside the caste even get killed by their own kin "to save the family honour". [11]

Often government interferences also muddy the waters. For instance, the Child Marriage (Amendment) Bill 2021 was introduced by the Indian cabinet in Parliament in December 2021. It aims to increase the minimum marriageable age of females from 18 to 21 years. Since a girl at 18 is otherwise considered an adult to drive, sign a contract and even vote, why must the state meddle with her right to cohabit? There is more to it; the Bill has since been sent to the Standing Committee of the Parliament for scrutiny which comprises, lo and behold, 30 male and solitary female lawmakers.

Viewed in its totality, in an increasingly feminist world, the institution of marriage, the very cornerstone of society, continues to remain heavily loaded against women – a classic case of good intentions hijacked by misguided practices and questionable laws.

Women are also disadvantaged when it comes to their Reproductive Rights signifying their choice to reproduce or to terminate an unwanted pregnancy. It also entails their right to plan a family and to choose the preferred method to do so. The Right also ensures their good health and economic well-being. While it is the state's responsibility to guarantee these Rights, countries have differing laws. Some allow abortion, some others only on medical grounds and some prohibit it altogether. Surprisingly, in a retrograde move, the USA has tightened its existing abortion laws. In a landmark verdict, on June 24, 2022, in one of the most divisive and bitterly fought issues, the US Supreme Court overturned its fifty-year-old ruling which was the basis for legal abortion across America. Women in so progressive a country have now lost their right to terminate an unwanted pregnancy without the government's unwelcome interference. There were widespread protests by women – one was seen carrying a poster that read "Leave my body alone." The poster conveyed it all.

According to the World Health Organization, one in three women experiences domestic violence or sexual abuse in their lifetime. Domestic violence could well be physical, verbal, financial, or maybe a case of total neglect. Its reporting by the victims remains poor for fear of social stigma. [12] Sexual abuse also takes many forms such as lewd comments and unwanted sexual advances besides of course rape. Unfortunately, quite often men think they are entitled to such acts. Worse still, some even tend to trivialize these grievous offenses. Here are three appalling comments on rape by three senior Indian leaders:- [13]

> ➢ As the Chief Minister of Haryana, Om Prakash Chautala was in favour of reducing the age of marriage to "curb the incidents of rape".

➢ Commenting on a rape case, in 2014, Mulayam Singh Yadav, former Chief Minister of Uttar Pradesh said "Boys will be boys, they make mistakes."

➢ Former Chief Minister of Madhya Pradesh, Babulal Gaur was of the opinion that "Rape is sometimes right."

While on the subject of rape a mention must also be made of the marital rape. Exception 2 of Section 375 of the Indian Penal Code reads "Sexual intercourse or sexual act by a man with his own wife, the wife being not under 15 years of age, is not rape". The law protects the husband and gives no right to the wife to say no. Has she no property rights on her own body? Is she legally less empowered than a sex worker who can refuse to entertain a customer? Delhi High Court gave a split verdict on the issue which is now before the SC.[14]

A genital mutilation is also a form of sexual abuse. Traditionally practiced and followed by many cultures throughout the world – essentially in the African and Middle East countries – there are no medical reasons and justifications for it.

To crown it all one often hears of such inhuman practices as female foeticide and India is one of the worst offenders.

Lastly, a word about the objectification of women. It is usual to objectify women for their physical appearance, beauty, and/or sex appeal. It seems to be embedded in our daily life – advertising agencies use them as attractive props to sell their products, and movies, TV programmes, and media for their engaging value addition. Quite a few sporting events also have a bevy of 'Cheer Girls' for the merriment of the spectators rather than to cheer the players. Internet is full of sites that carry photographs of uniformed women under such sexist captions as 'Military Beauties', 'Stunning Warriors', 'Sexy Female Soldiers', and so on. Female celebrities also often get viciously trolled, or get a raw deal for no fault of theirs – during the 2004 Super Bowl performance, Janet Jackson was blacklisted because of a wardrobe malfunction that left her breast exposed; but Justin Timberlake, her co-performer who caused it, went scot-free. Individually and collectively all such sexist orientations and exertions dehumanize women and push them to conform to the male narrative.

Wish List of the Eves

Women's wish list of hopes, ambitions, and goals is small but does convey their expectations in no uncertain terms. They want: -

- ➤ Men dominated society to change its mindset and treat them as equal though not identical.
- ➤ To be treated as equal in the personal, social, and professional domains.
- ➤ A far greater role in public life to moderate women's views and requirements to sensitize society and thus narrow down the existing gender gap.
- ➤ Equal opportunities and gender parity, including uniformity in pay, at the workplace.
- ➤ To be legally in control of their reproductive rights and associated health issues.
- ➤ A stop to all types of gender-based violence – sexual, physical, emotional, or financial – and also a stop to illogical and harmful traditional practices against them.
- ➤ Not to be objectified as a 'titillating item' and be treated as normal human beings.

Surely, for none of these can women be faulted for being overweening. Their wish list deserves to be addressed with supportive understanding, attitude, and behaviour.

In Sum

The preceding text is at best a short take on an extremely complicated facet of social engineering. While all the constitutions, laws, and policy guidelines profess equality of genders, the society, afflicted by toxic masculinity, fails to practice it. In spite of that, the issues of gender equality are now gaining traction all over the world. Though the progress in different regions and in different fields is uneven, women are inching forward towards a new order shored up by realism rather than idealism. The day they are treated as equal, without having to ape-men or to prove themselves, will be their finest hour. Alexander Dumas, arguably one of the greatest storytellers, thus concludes his masterly novel, *The Count of Monte Cristo* "There is neither happiness nor misery in the world; there is only the comparison of one state with another - - - Live, then, and be happy - - - all human wisdom is contained in two words, Wait and Hope."

TAILPIECE

Ladies, besides being homemakers nonpareil, you have made your mark in every single field that you have ventured into including in the most demanding and hazardous one of them all – the profession of arms. You have achieved much and you have the strength, motivation, and abilities to achieve much more. In the changing social landscape, the idea of women's empowerment has taken roots. Your silence has been heard. It is time for you to say 'let's go'. Yours is a 'work in progress'. Your story is still being written.

May you scale new heights and change the way the world perceives you. But do remain the woman that you are. You are an enigma wrapped in mystery. You symbolize fertility and motherhood. You nurture life. God has created you differently with many attributes superior to those of men.

Long live the difference.

Endnotes

1. Trevor Wilson, *The Myriad Faces of War,* Polity Press Cambridge, in Association with Basil Blackwell, Oxford, 1988, pp 716.

2. Kathleen Newland, *The Sisterhood of Man,* The Impact of Women's Changing Roles on Social and Economic Life Around the World, W W Norton & Company, New York, USA, First Edition, 1979, pp 203.

3. Dr. Om Raj Singh Vishnoi, *Women Police in India,* Aravali Printers, and Publishers (P) Ltd, New Delhi 1999, pp 15.

4. Women in all countries in the world now have voting rights. Last one to grant it was Saudi Arabia in 2015.

5. For details see https://worldpopulationreview.com/country-rankings/countries-with-female-leaders (accessed on May 20, 2022).

6. The Times of India (Delhi edition*), Iceland elects Europe's first female majority parliament,* September 27, 2021, pp 16. Recount reduced them down to 48%.

7. The Times of India (Delhi edition*), Felt hurt and alone as a woman:EU exec on Turkey chair snub,* April 28, 2021, pp 18.

8. The Times of India (Delhi edition), *Google to pay $118 m to 15K+ women staff over salary bias suit,* Jun 14, 2022, pp 13.

9. Ruchi Saini, Times of India (Delhi edition), *Having it all Redefined,* March 8, 2021, pp 14.

10. The Times of India (Delhi edition*), Women Say No,* May 15, 2021, pp 14.

11. For details see The Times of India (Delhi edition*), There is no honour in 'honour killings' so drop the prefix,* December 19, 2021, pp 24.

12. In India, National Family Health Survey – 5, for the year 2019-2020 found that as many as 77% of women never report.

13. See https://www.indiatoday.in/india/story/5-times-politicians-have-disgusted-us-with-rape-comments-1888922-2021-12-17, (Accessed on May 26, 2022)

14. Vrinda Bhandari, Why *Marital Rape Qualifies as Rape,* India Today, May 30, 2022, pp16.

Appendix A

THE WOMAN

When God created the woman, He was working late on the 6th day.

An angel came and asked, "Why spend so much time on it?"

Replied the Lord. "Did you see all the specifications I had to meet in order to design it?"

"She must function in all kinds of situations.
She must be able to adopt several children at once.
Have a hug that can heal anything from a bruised knee to a broken heart.
She must do it all with just two hands.
She heals herself when she is sick and can work 18 hours a day."

The angel was impressed. "Only two hands…. Impossible! And this is the standard model?"
The angel approached and touched the woman.
"But you made her so soft, Lord."

"She is soft," God said.
"But I made her strong. You cannot imagine what she can endure and overcome."

"Can she think?" asked the angel…

Replied the Lord, "Not only can she think, she can reason and negotiate."

The angel touched her cheek….
"God, this piece seems to be leaking! You have put too much of a burden on it."

"She's not leaking…… it is a tear." The Lord corrected the angel.

"What is it for?" asked the angel.

Said the Lord. "Tears are her way of expressing her sorrow, her doubts, her love, her loneliness, her suffering, and her pride."...

It made a great impression on the angel,
"God, you are a genius. You thought of everything. A truly wonderful woman."
Said the Lord "Indeed she is."
"She has the power to amaze a man.
She can handle troubles and carry heavy loads.
She holds happiness, love, and opinions.
She smiles when she feels like screaming.
She sings when she feels like crying, cries when she is happy, and laughs when she is scared.
She fights for what she believes in.
Her love is unconditional.
Her heart breaks when a relative or friend dies, but she finds the strength to continue living."

The angel asked, "So she is a perfect being?"

The Lord replied "No. She has only one drawback."
"She often forgets what she is worth."

- Devina Nund

Appendix B

BALLAD IN PRAISE OF PRIVATE CLARKE

With musket on her shoulder, her part she acted then,
And everyone supposed that she had been a man;
Her bandoleers about her neck, and sword hanged by her side,
In many brave adventures, her valour had been tried.

For other manly practices, she gained the love of all,
For leaping and for running or wrestling for a fall,
For cudgels or for cuffing, if that occasion were,
There's hardly any one of ten men that might with her compare.

Yet civil in her carriage and modest still was she,
But with her fellow soldiers she oft would merry be;
She would drink and take tobacco, and spend her money too,
When as occasion served that she had nothing else to do.

- Anon

Appendix C

A BRIEF EXPLANATION OF SOME OF THE TERMS OF LOW-INTENSITY CONFLICTS

Sub Conventional Operations

These operations are the ones that appear at the lower end of the spectrum of conflict – the upper end being nuclear warfare – and encompass all types of armed struggles that remain below the threshold of war. These include insurgencies, proxy wars, acts of terrorism, suicide attacks, and, in the Indian context, also the skirmishes along the disputed borders. These conflicts are invariably long-drawn-out struggles and are characterized by asymmetric warfare.

Asymmetric Warfare

Simply stated it means engagement between two unevenly matched and dissimilar forces. Though the term has become synonym with sub-conventional operations, it has relevance in all forms of warfare. Besides the force levels, the asymmetry could be in the relative goals, battle spaces, time dimensions, and the relative ethics (or the absence of it) in the trials of combat. Therein, whereas the armed forces are restrained by the rules of engagement and other socio-legal compulsions, the adversary thrives on disregarding such restrictions. The opponents try to exploit the divergent capabilities of the adversary to their own advantage.

Insurgency

Word insurgency originates from the Latin word 'insurgere' which in itself is an inflection of 'insurgo' meaning 'to rise up against'.

"A dissent of a group of people, who rise up against a lawfully constituted government, becomes an insurgency when it turns into an armed struggle. It springs when there is a festering grievance that the state fails to address. The struggle could be for political or socio-economic fulfillment and is sustained by the 'cause' that has mass public appeal. All insurgencies have an organizational and a hierarchical structure with a 'Political Wing' acting as the fountainhead of the movement, and a 'Military Wing' that carries out the arm-twisting acts of violence. An insurgency could be rural or urban. Whereas the aim of both insurrections is to overthrow the established government, the difference lies in their approach to do so -- a rural insurgency starts in remote areas and spreads to towns and cities, whereas urban insurgency aims to control centers of power to paralyze the countryside. In both the cases, active or tacit foreign support maybe there". [1]

Proxy War

Unlike insurgency, which is an armed struggle by a section of the local population against the state, a proxy war is initiated and sustained by a hostile nation using non-state actors to fight on its behalf in the target country. At the very least the hostile state provides ideological and financial support to these fighters. More often also arms and ammunition, training facilities, and safe havens besides of course also championing the 'cause' and the sacrifices of the fighters through print and electronic media. Thus, whereas India is combating insurgency in Manipur for example, it is up against Pakistan-sponsored proxy war in Jammu & Kashmir.

Terrorism

"Terrorism, often also referred to as '4th Generation Warfare' (4GW), is a prolonged and violent political struggle punctuated by high profile acts of terrorism. It is waged by non-state actors motivated by their misplaced politico-religious ideals. These brainwashed cadres consider themselves 'Freedom Fighters' or 'Soldiers of the God' and are ready to die for their 'cause'. Terror organizations do have a 'Master Mind' but usually no formal organizational structure. For their financial support, terrorist groups are mixed up with gun-running, drug trafficking, and money laundering mafias across the globe. They strike on all fronts – political, ideological, cultural, and religious. In 4GW therefore, there is a blurring of lines between war and politics and the soldiers and the civilians. Through psychological war and media manipulation, practitioners of the 4GW project the state as a bully. Their terror strikes convey to the political masters the high price to be paid. Their decentralized functioning in small entities deprives the state to deliver a crippling blow". [2]

Naxalism

The name has Indian roots. Terms Naxals, Naxalites, and Naxalism have originated from the Naxalbari Revolt of 1967 in West Bengal where the tribals rose against the repressive landlords over unfair land-grabbing and share-cropping practices. Their ideology has remained much in the manner of Mao Zedong's political thoughts of 'Protracted People's War'. In 2004 it joined hands with others to form the Communist Party of India (Maoist) with the objective of establishing a 'Red Corridor' starting from Bihar and running across the states of Jharkhand, Orissa, Chhattisgarh, Andhra Pradesh, Maharashtra and Karnataka.

Radicalization

The term finds its origin in the Latin word *Radix* meaning root but generally implies something that is basic or fundamental. Though widely discussed and debated after the terror strikes and suicide attacks of the last few decades, the term has thus far defied a generally accepted definition. In simple words, it refers to a gradual process by which an individual or a group adopts, or is mentored to adopt, increasingly extreme views and stand on political, ideological, religious, or socio-economic issues – a slippery slope that leads to violent activities.

Endnotes

1. Major General V K Shrivastava, *MANTHAN*, Vij Books India Pvt Ltd, New Delhi, India, 2021, pp 47-48.

2. Ibid, pp 48-49.

Appendix D

ACTUAL STRENGTH OF WOMEN (ALL RANKS) IN VARIOUS UNITS/BRANCHES OF INDIAN CIVIL POLICE (AS ON JANUARY 1, 2020)

1.	Women civil police in states/ UTs	1,74,716.
2.	Women in District Armed Reserve in States/UTs	20,391.
3.	Women in Special Armed Police Battalion in states/UTs	14,401.
4.	Women in Indian Reserve Battalion in states/UTs	5888.
5.	Women in Commando Battalion in states/UTs	426.
6.	Women in Traffic Police in states/UTs	5979.
7.	Women in Special Branch (Intelligence) in states/UTs	3632.
8.	Women in Crime Investigation Department in states/UTs	1940.
9.	Women in Special Operations Police Unit in states/UTs	516.
Grand Total		**2,27,889.**

(**Source.** Publication by Bureau of Police Research and Development, *Data on Police Organizations, (as on January 1, 2020),* New Delhi, 2021, pp 95-129.)

Appendix E

ACTUAL STRENGTH OF WOMEN (ALL RANKS) IN INDIA'S CENTRAL ARMED POLICE FORCES
(AS ON JANUARY 1, 2020)

1.	Assam Rifles	953.
2.	Border Security Force	5139.
3.	Central Industrial Security Force	8631.
4.	Central Reserve Police Force	7860.
5.	Indo-Tibetan Border Police	2023.
6.	Sashastra Seema Bal	2080.
7.	National Disaster Response Force	122.
8.	National Security Guards	106.
9.	Railway Protection Force	2335.
Grand Total		**29,249.**

(**Note.** Serials 1 to 7 are under the Ministry of Home Affairs, 8 is under the Prime Minister's Office and Serial 9 is under the Ministry of Railways.)

(**Source.** Publication by Bureau of Police Research and Development, *Data on Police Organizations, (as on January 1, 2020),* New Delhi, 2021, pp 140 – 142.)

Appendix F

THERE ARE NO GENDER-NEUTRAL BATTLEFIELDS

A battlefield is an unforgiving place. It does not understand decency and civilized behaviour, and it does not give consideration to physical or physiological differences.

Mountains do not become any less steep, nor does the enemy stop firing because the adversary is not a male like him.

Simply because the female soldier underwent diluted standards of physical fitness tests in the academy does not give her the right to slow down her comrades nor compromise their safety because she cannot keep pace with them.

It does not give her the right to seek privileges or special dispensations on account of her gender, because she has already demanded and been given equality when she demanded her right to enter the battlefield.

I am not for a moment suggesting that women are weak or unfit for battle. Our female athletes have displayed their prowess in the sports arena time and again. But in the stadium, her opponents are of the same gender, and there are rules that are strictly followed. The battlefield does not have such niceties. There are no referees nor any appeals. Might is right and the means don't matter.

But if the honourable Supreme Court with its supreme wisdom opines that women are indeed equal to men and are fit for battle, then who are we to think otherwise? Let us accept their diktat gracefully.

But for the sake of the men that they will command, and for the sake of the eventual security of the nation, let it be a level playing field for men and women alike. Let the selection process, requirements and physical standards be the same regardless of gender. As an example, consider the minimum height for a male candidate for joining the OTA, the stipulation for which is presumably based on the envisaged job requirements. Why should a male be at least

157.5 cm in height but a female is acceptable if she is 152 cm? Why should a Gentleman Cadet running 2.4 km in 10 minutes be rated "satisfactory" but a Lady Cadet doing the same run in 12 minutes be graded "excellent"? Where is the logic in this? Are we training them for different battlefields and different adversaries?

Lest I be branded as a narrow-minded male chauvinist, let us view this issue from a different perspective. Let us assume that the male and the female are truly equal in the battlefield and we have achieved gender equality by inducting women officers. The question now arises, are we not now indulging in socio-economic discrimination? Why only officers? Why not a similar opportunity for female soldiers. Throw open the doors for recruitment of women in every regimental centre. Let every infantry battalion, every armoured and artillery regiment be completely gender-neutral. Otherwise, we are simply catering to the educated elite while neglecting the aspirations of other segments of society. And while at it, what about transgenders? Why are they being discriminated against? After all, history tells us that eunuchs were widely employed as security guards for harems in palaces.

The Chetwode motto says "The safety, honour and welfare of your country come first, always and every time". My sincere request to the honourable Court and other advocates for equality is, please pay heed to these wise words. The safety, honour and welfare of the country are far too precious, far too hard-earned to let it be compromised on the whims of those who are far removed from the reality of war. And my sincere request to the senior hierarchy of the military establishment is, please follow the Chetwode credo. Stand up for what is right. Do not forget that "your own ease, comfort and safety come last, always and every time". Your subordinates will pay with their blood for the compromises that you make today.

Think about it. Jai Hind.

(Note. This widely circulated WhatsApp message was received by the author in August 2022. The writer's name was not mentioned therein.)

BIBLIOGRAPHY

Chapter - 1

1. Ainslie T Embree (Ed), *Sources of Indian Tradition*, Second edition, Penguin Books India(P) Ltd, 1991.

2. Jawahar Lal Nehru, *Discovery of India,* Oxford University Press, Eighteenth Impression, 1998.

3. Dr C P Ramaswami Aiyer, *The Cultural Heritage oh India,* Volume-II, First Edition, The Ramakrishna Mission Institute of Culture, Calcutta, 1962.

4. Annada Sankar Ray, *An Outline of Indian Culture,* Intellectual Book Corner, New Delhi, 1978.

5. Helena Rosenblatt, *The Lost History of Liberalism : From Ancient Rome to the Twenty-First Century*, Princeton University Press, 2018.

Chapter - 2

1. Jonathan Bastable, Antony Mason, Tony Allen, *Reader's Digest : Great Secrets of History*, Therefore Publishing House, Brighton, U K, 2014.

2. Julian Spilsbury, *The Indian Mutiny*, Weidenfeld & Nicolson, London, 2007

Chapter - 3

1. M. C. Devilbiss, *Women and Military Service : A History, Analysis, and Overview of Key Issues,* Air University Press Maxwell Air Force Base, Alabama USA, 1990.

2. Andrew de la Garza, *Mughals at War: Babur, Akbar, and the Indian Military Revolution, 1500 - 1605,* The Ohio State University,

USA, 2010.

3. D Collette Wadge (Ed), *Women in Uniform,* Sampson Low, Martson and Co, Ltd, 1946.

Chapter - 4

1. Angela Bolton, *The Maturing Sun: An Army Nurse inn India, 1942-45,* Imperial War Museum book Distributed by Jane's Publishing Company, London, UK, 1986.

2.. Professor R S Kaushala, *Women Warriors : Brave Deeds Done by Women in 2 Great Wars,* The Standard Publishing Co, Ambala City, India, First Edition,1944.

3.* Rita James Simon (Ed), *Women in the Military,* Transaction Publishers, New Brunswick (USA) and London (UK), 1998. *

4.* Margaret Randolph Hingonnet, Jane Jenson, Sonya Michel, Margaret Collins Weitz (Ed), *Behind the Lines : Gender and the Two World Wars,* Yale University Press, New Haven and London, 1987.*

5.. Trevor Wilson, *The Myriad Faces of War,* Polity Press Cambridge, in Association with Basil Blackwell, Oxford, 1988.

6.. G J Meyer, *A World Undone : The Story of the Great War, 1914-1918,* Bantam Dell New York, 2006.

Chapter - 5

1. M R Narayan Swami, *The Tiger Vanquished : LTTE's Story,* SAGE Publications India Pvt Ltd, New Delhi, India, 2010.

2. Arpita Anant (ed), *Non-State Armed Groups In South Asia : A Preliminary Structured Focused Comparison,* Pentagon Security International, New Delhi, India, 2012.

3. Rahul Pandita, *Hello Bastar : The Untold Story of India's Maoist Movement,* Tranquebar Press, New Delhi, India, 2011.

4. V N Singh, Naxalism : A Great Menace, Prashant Publishing House, New Delhi, India, 2010.

5. Lt Gen Gautam Banerjee, *Reign of the Red Rebellion : Observa-*

tions From Naxal Land, Lancer Publishers and Distributors, New Delhi, India, 2013.

6. P V Ramana (ed), The Naxal Challenge : Causes, Linkages and policy Options, Dorling KIndersley (India) Pvt Ltd, New Delhi, India, 2008.

7. Rasmi Saksena, *She Goes to War : Women Militants of India,* Speaking Tiger Publishing, Pvt Ltd, New Delhi, India, 2018.

Chapter - 6

1. S K Pandit, *Women in Society,* Rajat Publications, New Delhi, 1998.

2. Lt Col M D Sharma, *Para Military Forces of India,* Kalpaz publications, Delhi, 2008.

3. Subhash Joshi, IPS, Rekha Pande, *Gender Issues and Police in India : A Report,* Sardar Vallabhbhai Patel National Police Academy, 1999.

4. National Police Research Repository : Research Studies on Police and Prison Issues (1970 – 2016), Published by Bureau of Police Research and Development, New Delhi, 2017.

5. National Police Research Repository, Golden Jubilee Edition : Research Studies on Police and Prison Issues (2016 – 2020), Published by Bureau of Police Research and Development, New Delhi, 2021.

6. Anirudh Deshpande (Ed), *Glorious Fifty years of Border Security Force,* Shipra Publication, Delhi, India, 2015.

7. R S D Dogra, *Securing the Nation : Central Reserve Police (CRPF),* Manas Publication, New Delhi, 2001.

8. Om Raj Singh Vishnoi, *Women Police in India,* Aravali Printers and Publishers (P) Ltd, New Delhi, India, 1999.

9. Aruna Bhardwaj, *Women in Uniform : Emergence of Women Police in India.* Regency Publications, New Delhi, India,1999,

Chapter - 7

1. Tom Bowden, *Army in the Service of the State*, University Publishing Projects, Tel Aviv, Israel, 1976.

2. Benjamin Lai, *The Dragon's Teeth*, Casemate, Publishers, Havertown, PA, USA.

3. Philip C Saunders, Arther S Ding, Andrew Scobell, Andrew ND and Joel Wuthnow (Ed), *Chairman Xi Remakes the PLA : Assessing Chinese Military Reforms,* National Defence University Press, USA, 2019, (Published in India by Alpha Editions).

Chapter - 8

1. Anand Ballabh, *Recruitment and Training in Indian Armed Forces,* Forward Books, New Delhi, 2013.

2. A C Bhaktivedanta Swami Prabhupada, *Bhagvada Geeta As It Is,* Bhaktivedanta Book Trust, Mumbai 1998.

3. Rajesh Kadian, *India and its Army*, Vision Books Pvt Ltd, New Delhi, 1990.

Chapter - 9

1. Stuart A Cohen (Ed), *Democratic Societies And Their Armed Forces : Israel In Comparative Context*, Frank Cass Publishers, London, UK, 2000.

2. Anuradha M Chenoy, *Militarism & Women in South Asia*, Kali for Women, New Delhi, India, 2002.

3.* Nicole Detraz, *International Security and Gender*, Polity Press, Cambridge, UK, 2012. *

4. Lionel Tiger, *Men in Groups*, Transaction Publishers, New Jersey, USA,1969.

Chapter - 10

1.* Kathleen Newland, *The Sisterhood of Man, The Impact of Women's Changing Roles on Social and Economic Life Around the World,* W W Norton & Company, New York, USA, First Edition, 1979. *

2.* Tsjeard Bouta, Georg Frerks, Ian Bannon, *Gender, Conflict and Development*, The World Bank, Washington DC, USA, 2005. *

Journals and Articles

1. Publication by Bureau of Police Research and Development, *Data on Police Organizations, (As on January 1, 2020)*, New Delhi, 2021.

2. Maj Gen Mrinal Suman, AVSM, VSM, Phd, *Women in the Indian Armed Forces*, Indian Defence Review, Jul-Sep 2006, Vol 21.

3. Dr Meena Dutta, *Women in Armed Forces : A Leadership Perspective*, Pinnacle, 2014, Vol 13.

4. Suvarna Joshi, *The State of Women Police in India and the Discrimination Faced by Them*, The International Journal of Indian Psychology, Volume 2, Issue 4, July – September, 2015.

5. Major General Mrinal Suman, AVSM, VSM, (Retd), *Women in the Armed Forces : Misconceptions and Facts*, USI Journal, 2010, Jan-Mar, Vol 140.

6. Sabine T. Koeszegi, Eva Zedlacher, and Rene´ Hudribusch, *The War Against the Female Soldier? The Effects of Masculine Culture on Workplace Aggression*, Armed Forces & Society 2014, Vol. 40(2) 226-251, Reprints and permission: sagepub.com/journalsPermissions.nav.

7. Connie Brownson, *The Battle for Equivalency : Female US Marines Discuss Sexuality, Physical Fitness, and Military Leadership*, Armed Forces & Society 2014, Vol. 40(4) 765-788, Reprints and permission: sagepub.com/journalsPermissions.nav.

8. Anthony C. King, *Women Warriors : Female Accession to Ground Combat, Armed Forces & Society*, 2015, Vol.41(2) 379-387, Reprints and permission: sagepub.com/journalsPermissions.nav.

9. India Strategic, Vol 17, Issue 1, January 2022, New Delhi, India.

10. Claire Duncanson, Rachel Woodward, *Regendering the military: Theorizing women's military participation*, Security Dialogue 2016, Vol. 47(1) 3–21, Reprints and permissions: sagepub.co.uk/journalsPermissions.nav.

11. Connie Brownson, *Rejecting Patriarchy for Equivalence in the US Military: A Response to Anthony King's "Women Warriors: Female Accession to Ground Combat"* Armed Forces & Society 2016, Vol. 42(1) 235-242 Reprints and permission: sagepub.com/journalsPermissions.nav.

Internet

Websites as quoted.

INDEX

A

Agni Pariksha 7

Ahilya Bai Holkar 17

Alka Khurana, Capt 71

American Civil War 16

American Revolutionary War 22

Andaman Islands 2

Archana Ramachandran 57

Ardhangini 7

Arjuna awardees 55

  Bharti Singh 55

  Chhaya Adak 55

  Shilpi Singh 55

Army Nursing Service 24, 25

Artemis 5, 13

Arthashastra 8

B

Battle of Elephant Pass 42

Battle of Monmouth 23

Battle of Somme 29

Bharti Singh 55

Black Tigers 44

Boko Haram 45

C

Cachar Levy 52

Centre for Military Readiness 79

Chand Bibi 19

Chechnya 44, 45

Chinese Communist Party xi, 63

Chinese Joan of Arc 41. *See also* Qui Jin

Christian Cavanagh 15

Claire Lacombe 40

Communist Party of India (Maoist) xi, 42, 102

Cordon and Search Operations 52

COVID-19 iii

Crimean War 23, 24

D

Daniel Defoe 15

Deepika Misra, Sqn Ldr 71

Doctrine of Lapse 17, 20

Draupadi 7

Dukhataran-i-Millat 43

Durga 7

E

East India Company xi, 17, 20

English Civil War 15

F

Fatma Omar al-Najar 45

First Aid Nursing Yeomanry xi, 30

First World War 25, 28, 30, 33, 34, 37, 50, 78

Florence Nightingale 24

French Revolution 40

G

Gandharva Vivah 6

Garuda Commandos 57

Gaza Strip 44

Golda Mier 87

Greek phalanx 8

Greek Queen Artemisia 13

Gulf War 61

Gunjan Saxena, Flt Lt 71, 75

H

Hall of Fame 30

Hamas 45

I

Indian National Army xi, 19

Indira Nooyi 89

Indo-Pak conflict 53

Indo-Tibetan Border Police 57, 104

Indus Valley Civilization 6

Ishtar 5

Islamic State of Iraq and Syria 45, 66

J

Jarawa tribe 2

Jauhar 9

Jhalkari Bai 18

K

Khawateen Markaz 43

Kiran Bedi 51

Kit Welsh 15

Korean War 61

Kristina Dmitrenko 66

Kshatriya 8, 69

Kshatriyas 8

L

Lady with the Lamp 24

Lakshmi Bai 17, 18

Liberation Tigers of Tamil Eelam xii, 42

Lord Wavell 69

Loreta Janeta Velázquez 15, 16

M

Mahabharat 7, 8, 69

Manusmrity 7

Margarita Neri 41

Maria Antonia Santos Plata 41

Mariam Mansouri 66

Marie Owens 50

Martin Van Creveld 81

Mary Churchill 33

Mata Hari 32, 37

Minerva 5

Muhammad Ali Jinnah 64

N

National Defence Academy xii, 72

National Security Guards 57, 104

Naxal movement 42, 56

Neolithic Age 3

New Stone Age 2

Nigar Johar 65

Nightingale School for Nurses 24

Nike 5

Nikhat Zareen 89

Noor Inayat Khan 35

Normandy 34

North Atlantic Treaty Organization 66

O

Officers Training Academy 70

Oshrat Bachar 63

P

People's Liberation Army xii, 43, 63

People's Liberation Guerrilla Army 43

Phoolan Devi 46

Prabhakaran 42

Q

Queen Alexandra's Imperial Nursing Service 25

Qui Jin 41. *See also* Chinese Joan of Arc

R

Ramayana 7, 8

Rani Durgavati 16

Rani Velu Nachiyar 17

Rann of Kuchh 53

Rashtriya Indian Military College xii, 73

Road Opening Party 52

Royal Navy xii, 25, 30

Roza Shanina 34

Ruchi Sharma, Capt 71

S

Sandinista National Liberation Front 44

Sashastra Seema Bal 57, 104

Second World War 32, 33, 36, 44, 60, 61, 78

Sexual dimorphism 1, 79

Shilpi Singh 55

Siachen Glacier 80

Subhadra Kumari Chauhan 18

Subhas Chandra Bose 18

Sun Tzu 77

Swayamwara 6

T

Tanu Shree Pareek 54

Tara Bai 17

The Jewish Revolt 40

The Night Witches 34

U

United Liberation Front of Assam xii, 43

Upanishads 6

V

Vedic period 6

Venus 5, 79

Vietnam War 61

W

William Howard Russell 23

Women in the Indian Police Service 50

Women Protection Cell 51

Women's Royal Air Force xii, 30

Women's Royal Navy Service xii, 30

ABOUT THE AUTHOR

An alumnus of the National Defence Academy, Khadakwasla, he was commissioned in 1962 into the infantry – Rajputana Rifles – the cutting edge of soldiering.

He was in J&K during the Indo-Pak conflict of 1965 and was in Bangladesh in the 1971 war. A graduate of the Defence Services Staff College, Wellington, he also attended the prestigious National Defence College, New Delhi. He has held a number of coveted command, staff and instructional appointments and was awarded Vishishta Seva Medal for his distinguished services while combating insurgency in northeast India.

Post-retirement in 1998 he had a short stint as the Executive Editor of the Indian Defence Review before Joining the Institute for Defence Studies and Analyses, New Delhi, as a Senior Fellow. From there he led many delegations for interactions with think tanks abroad and was also a member of the Indian team invited by the National Defence University, USA, for strategic dialogue.

He has written researched text for four coffee table books, has a published monograph on China, a prize-winning essay, and a number of articles on matters military to his credit. His latest book, "Manthan: Multifaceted Reflections on the Indian Armed Forces", was released in Feb 2021.

CPSIA information can be obtained
at www.ICGtesting.com
Printed in the USA
LVHW111250101122
732762LV00005B/226